Résumés
COVER
LETTERS
Networking
& Interviewing

FOURTH EDITION

Clifford W. Eischen

Fresno City College

Lynn A. Eischen

Eischen's Professional Résumé Service

SOUTH-WESTERN
CENGAGE Learning

Australia • Brazil • Japan • Korea • Mexico • Singapore • Spain • United Kingdom • United States

SOUTH-WESTERN
CENGAGE Learning

Résumés, Cover Letters, Networking, and Interviewing, Fourth Edition
Clifford W. Eischen and Lynn A. Eischen

Vice President of Editorial, Business: Jack W. Calhoun

Publisher: Erin Joyner

Acquisitions Editor: Jason Fremder

Developmental Editor: Jennifer King

Editorial Assistant: Megan Fischer

Marketing Manager: Michelle Lockard

Senior Marketing Communications Manager: Sarah Greber

Marketing Coordinator: Leigh Taylor Smith

Production Management, and Composition: PreMediaGlobal

Media Editor: John Rich

Rights Acquisition Director: Audrey Pettengill

Rights Acquisition Specialist, Text and Image: Sam Marshall

Manufacturing Planner: Ron Montgomery

Senior Art Director: Stacy Shirley

Cover Designer: Lou Ann Thesing

Cover Image: © iStock Images

© 2013, 2010, 2007 South-Western, Cengage Learning

For product information and technology assistance, contact us at **Cengage Learning Customer & Sales Support, 1-800-354-9706**

For permission to use material from this text or product, submit all requests online at **www.cengage.com/permissions** Further permissions questions can be emailed to **permissionrequest@cengage.com**

Library of Congress Control Number: 2011939235

ISBN-13: 978-1-111-82084-8

ISBN-10: 1-111-82084-8

South-Western
5191 Natorp Boulevard
Mason, OH 45040
USA

Cengage Learning products are represented in Canada by Nelson Education, Ltd.

For your course and learning solutions, visit **www.cengage.com**

Purchase any of our products at your local college store or at our preferred online store **www.cengagebrain.com**

Printed in the United States of America
1 2 3 4 5 6 7 8 16 15 14 13 12

DEDICATION

To my former students at Fresno City College and the Technical University of Budapest who provided the inspiration to write and pursue excellence in teaching and academics. Several former students continue to enrich our lives; we greatly value their support and friendship. We would like to recognize three students: Eric Olson, Keith Kompsi, and Istvan Godri. Thank you for being part of our lives. We take great joy in watching each of you grow in your careers and in becoming valued fathers and members of your communities.

PREFACE

The material in this text takes a step-by-step approach in the development of professional résumés and career marketing materials. Résumé writing is not difficult; however, it does take considerable time to create an attention-getting résumé. It requires some word processing ability and a focus on the skills desired by employers. The key to every good résumé is research, attractive layout, and numerous drafts. This book will help you develop a résumé that you may proudly present to prospective employers. It will teach you how to prepare résumés for e-mailing, mailing, faxing, and posting to job boards and company sites. We have provided abundant examples of résumés, cover letters, letters of recommendation, follow-up letters, salary histories, reference pages, examples of business skills, and networking techniques. This book will also demonstrate how to conduct employer research via the Internet and prepare answers to potential interview questions.

The fourth edition includes many additions and enhancements, including a focus on using social networks to improve one's opportunities in discovering positions of interest that are often not published, digital résumé preparation and submission, researching prospective employers online, and Internet sources that highlight job openings. All résumé examples have been modified and updated. The first chapter contains a sample résumé for critiquing by readers to assess their proofreading skills and knowledge of résumé preparation. Additional focus has been added to emphasize how critical résumé appearance is in making an initial impact on a prospective employer.

Just as technology has changed how we communicate, so have résumés changed. We now post résumés on job boards or on a website, send them via e-mail and fax, and often provide a résumé as an e-mail attachment. For now the vehicle of choice for job seekers and employers is the well-written, professional-appearing résumé—whether it be in digital or printed format. We have simplified this process and wish you well as you embark on your career search using the tools and strategies found in this publication.

In writing this text we are deeply indebted to the following colleagues and thankful for their contributions, editing, and encouragement:

Gigi Hill, formerly Chief Copy Editor, ABC Television

We would also like to thank the reviewers who provided significant suggestions on the ongoing development of this text:

Dave Aiken, Hocking College
Jonathan Grollman, Mount Ida College
Michelle Bresso, Bakersfield College
Donna Hendricks, South Arkansas Community College
Cindy Oakley-Paulik, Embry Riddle Aeronautical University
Shavawn Berry, Arizona State University

Lowell Habel, Concordia University
Andrea Feldman, University of Colorado

In addition, we would like to compliment the staff at South-Western/Cengage Learning for their professionalism in bringing this edition to completion. This includes Erin Joyner, Jason Fremder, Jennifer King, Michelle Lockard, Leigh Taylor Smith, Stacy Shirley, Megan Fischer, and all who contributed to this project.

Lynn and Cliff Eischen

Note to Instructors

Please note that both an Instructor's Manual and Test Bank accompany this text. The Instructor's Manual is filled with teaching strategies and additional information that will enrich the learning experience. The Test Bank, designed to make your test preparation easier, features ten multiple choice and two essay questions for each chapter.

ABOUT THE AUTHORS

Since 1972, Cliff and Lynn Eischen have prepared résumés professionally in a firm located in Fresno, California, where they have assisted literally thousands of job seekers with the preparation of their résumés. In addition, Cliff has taught résumé writing at Fresno City College for more than 30 years and given numerous seminars regarding résumé writing, developing interview skills, networking, utilizing the Internet in job searches, and human relations. His many years of experience teaching students to prepare résumés and cover letters and assisting them with interviewing techniques have resulted in this text. Cliff and Lynn Eischen have honed their résumé-writing and career-coaching skills from a multitude of professional sources and attendance at seminars provided by the National Résumé Writers Association (NRWA). They are members of NRWA and Cliff is certified by this organization. He is one of 30 writers designated as a Nationally Certified Résumé Writer (NCRW) by the NRWA whose membership numbers 430. Lynn received her certification from the Professional Association of Résumé Writers.

CONTENTS

CHAPTER 4
Essentials and Examples in Résumé Presentation   28

CHAPTER 5
Résumé Formats, Styles, and Applications   46

CHAPTER 6
Researching Prospective Employers Online and Tips on Salary Negotiations   52

Résumés
COVER
LETTERS
Networking
&Interviewing

FOURTH EDITION

Getting the Interview

Learning Objectives

1. Why do employers often want to see a résumé, even in addition to an application?
2. What is critical in the content and appearance of a résumé if you want an employer to read the entire résumé and call you for an interview?
3. What types of errors or omissions in a résumé might screen out a well-qualified candidate resulting in the applicant not being called for an interview?

THE SCREENING PROCESS—MAKING THE CUT

The purpose of a résumé is to allow potential employers the opportunity to find out as much as possible about your qualifications in a few minutes, maybe even seconds, to determine if they would like to meet with you. This decision will often be made on the basis of reviewing a few sheets of paper—your résumé, cover letter, and perhaps an application that you have submitted to the employer via e-mail, fax, the Internet, or "snail" mail.

Please look at the job posting for a medical assistant position that follows this paragraph, and then examine the résumé on the next (opposite) page. Review the résumé as though the applicant were a friend of yours who had given you the job announcement and her résumé to obtain your opinion as to whether the résumé is appropriate for this position. You might also imagine yourself as an employer trying to determine whether the résumé displays the qualifications required in the job announcement, and whether you would call the applicant for an interview. *After reviewing the résumé carefully, as part of Exercise 1.1, answer the 15 questions* that follow the résumé. After you have completed this exercise your instructor will provide you with information regarding any errors contained in the résumé as well as suggestions regarding its formatting and content.

MEDICAL ASSISTANT Front office position in busy office with 3 M.D.s. Skills required: greeting patients, scheduling, multi-line telephone system, MS Office Suite, e-mail/Internet, filing and office procedures, typing 40 WPM, and familiarity with Medical Manager. Salary dependent on training, experience, and skills. Full benefits. Fax résumé to 330-847-9210 or e-mail Word document to: Sherrie@ medicalgroup.com.

EXERCISE 1.1 REVIEW OF RÉSUMÉ

BARBARA S. PETERSON

3670 East Burns, Canton, OH 44720
(330) 494-6170

* *

Medical Office Job Desired

* *

Education:

Certificate of Completion - Medical Assistant Program 2012
     Stark State College of Technology, Canton, OH
Certified Nursing Assistant Program, Peabody Polytechnic High School, Amarillo, TX   2010

Internship - Nursing Assistant, Sierra View Convalescent, Amarillo, TX   2010

SKILLS/ABILITIES:

- Able to take patient histories and vitol signs; give injections; and perform intake charting, E.K.G.s, suture removal, throat cultures, specimen collection/handling, and transfer of nonambulatory patients.
- Experienced in completing tax forms and communicating discrepancies to taxpayers.
- Current CPR and First Aid Certifications.
- Language skills include ability to read, write, and speak Hungarian.
- E-mail and Internet experience very limited.
- Experience preparing CRF and source documentation utilized in billing insurance; copying, filing, and transfering medical records; and preparing patient charts.
- Skilled in medical terminology with Mestamed and Medical Manager Software.
- Computer proficent in MS Word and Excel.
- Received first place award for Needlepoint from Amarillo home and garden club.
- Multi-line phone experience screening patient calls and scheduling appointments.
- Possess excellent patient relations skills: friendly, patient, and aggressive.

Experience:

Clerk (part-time)
Internal Revenue Service, Amarillo, TX   2008–2011

Medical Assistants, Peachwood Medical Group, Amarillo, TX   2010–2012

Medical Supply Specialist, United States Army Reserve
 Combat Support Hospital Unit, Amarilo, TX   2008–2012

- *Training:* Quartermaster School, Medical Supply Special, Fort Lee, Virginia

1. How does the résumé look in general? Is it approximately centered? Can it be read easily? Is it appealing to the eye?
2. Is the spacing consistent throughout? Is the font size consistent? Are the sections/headings lined up and consistent in style?
3. After looking at it carefully, what suggestions would you make regarding layout changes?
4. Are there grammar, style, and organization errors in the résumé?
5. What stands out in the résumé? Are the items or sections that stand out important in view of what is requested in the job announcement?
6. Is all the contact information (name, address, phone, e-mail, etc.) that an employer would desire contained in the résumé?
7. What does the applicant want to do—what specific job/s is she seeking?
8. Are any words or terms misspelled? Is this important? Why?
9. Is there information contained in the résumé that should be omitted because it is not relevant to the position being sought? List those items that are insignificant.
10. What are the applicant's strongest qualifications? What qualifications requested in the advertisement are missing? Is it okay to omit skills desired by the employer if you do not have them?
11. How old is the applicant? Should this information be included in a résumé?
12. Should a cover letter also be written to accompany the résumé? What should it contain that is not included in the résumé?
13. Nothing is said about references; should references be part of the résumé?
14. Are there any time gaps in employment or school history? Employers look at this very carefully. Do you know why?
15. If you were an employer, what information on the résumé would you verify? Why? Did you know studies indicate that from 40 to 50 percent of all résumés have some information that is inaccurate?

An Employer's Perspective on Résumés

My former dentist told me of his first experience in advertising for a front-office assistant in his practice. He placed an advertisement in the local newspaper, and since he wanted to see the applicants in person he included his address and phone number. Well, on the Monday morning after the ad appeared on Sunday, more than 75 job seekers swarmed his office seeking an application and interview. He had so many applicants appear that there were no seats in the reception area for his patients. He said, "Never again will I put my address and phone number in an advertisement. I will list only an e-mail address or post office box for applicants to submit a résumé. I will use the résumé to screen the applicants and then call those that appear most qualified."

Employers review résumés of applicants with the idea of eliminating those who present themselves poorly, lack experience, or do not possess the required skills. This is similar to what we do when we first meet new friends or acquaintances. We look at them, their clothes, posture, smile, laugh, eyes, and so on, and then decide whether we would like to get to know them better. Our evaluation of them is based upon whether the qualities they possess are similar to those we value. In other words, if the first time we meet someone we see that he has a pleasant smile, laughs easily, and likes spending time outdoors, we might want to get to know him better—especially if we like people who are positive, have a good sense of humor, and enjoy hiking.

Employers do the same thing. They look for *qualities you possess that are valued in their businesses*. The characteristics they value are usually a consistent work history, positive attitude, related work experience, formal education, and training in areas where they have a specific need. An example for an administrative assistant would be word processing, filing, greeting customers, answering the telephone, and conducting research on the Internet. If they determine that you have most of these skills, they will probably want to interview you to see if you are someone they want to consider for possible employment in their company.

APPEARANCE IS CRITICAL

Be aware that it is not just the skills listed on your résumé that are important. It is much more than the written words you place on the résumé page or in the cover letter that are considered important. The *appearance* of the résumé and cover letter is critical. Like the fascinating person across the room at a party, *initially it is her appearance* that makes her seem interesting. The qualities that attract you to another individual are sometimes definable and sometimes not. However, in a résumé we can usually identify the characteristics that make it appealing to the reader.

Initially, your résumé's appearance will have the greatest impact on the reader/employer. The paper that you choose (quality and color), the placement on the paper (whether it is centered), the typeface and font size, spelling and punctuation, headings, length of previous jobs, and communication skills (choice of words and use of key words—words or technical language that indicate you are trained/knowledgeable in your field) will all be reviewed by the reader. Most employers *will look for an error or something missing in your background to screen out candidates* who do not possess the qualities they seek. After the initial impression and upon reading the cover letter, résumé, and application (and this will only occur if the reader likes what she has initially seen), the reader will begin to look at the organization of your material, your skills, experience, and education. And in the case of the cover letter, she will also look at the tone of your letter—meaning its attitude and whether it is positive and reasonably well written. From that first impression an employer will decide whether she wants to get to know you better—have a first meeting with you and conduct an initial interview.

WHAT YOU MUST DO IN PREPARING A RÉSUMÉ

Because a professional appearance is critical, it is appropriate to do the following:

1. Prepare your résumé on a computer using a laser or quality inkjet printer (the printed typeface should be clean and precise, not fuzzy). It is best to use a word processing program such as Microsoft Word or Corel WordPerfect so that your résumé can be modified and/or updated easily. Often you will want to modify the résumé when applying for a specific position, perhaps to include the exact title of the position and the company name. Also, you may think of some project or skill that you possess but initially omitted in the first draft of the résumé. Therefore, it is essential to have your résumé stored on a hard drive or memory stick for later modification.
2. The body of the text on the page should appear centered—both vertically and horizontally. It does not have to be measured precisely, but simply look centered when viewed by the naked eye.
3. Use the spell-check feature of the word processing program. Remember, every technical or business product name (like Intel or Linksys), plus the names of individuals, should be double-checked for accuracy as the spell-check feature of most software programs may not recognize any misspellings in these.
4. Have a friend, maybe two, with a formal education and/or a college degree proofread your résumé.
5. Complete the résumé several days before you need it. Doing it at midnight the day before you have an 8 a.m. interview often results in shoddy work.

6. When submitting a printed copy of your résumé as opposed to a digital résumé, use white, light gray, or ivory 24-pound classic laid or linen stationery of good quality.

RÉSUMÉ EXAMPLES

To illustrate how important appearance is, look at Figures 1.1 and 1.2 on the following pages. Both figures are identical in content (they are the same résumé); however, the formatting (appearance) of Figure 1.1 is professional in appearance, while Figure 1.2 is unacceptable because of improper spacing, centering, and layout—not because of content or typographical errors. Remember: *The presentation of your material is as important as what you write about yourself.* The résumé represents you at your best; therefore, look your best.

In addition, we have added two examples of résumés, Figures 1.3 and 1.4, at the end of this chapter for those who have completed a four-year degree but lack significant employment experience. The styles and formats for these résumés are representative of what often is contained in the marketing materials for those entering the job market after completing their bachelor's degree.

Figure 1.1 Professional Appearance

Rafael E. Cortez

5559 E. Spruce Ave.
Clovis, CA 93611
(559) 845-9621
rec559@aol.com

OBJECTIVE	*Administrative Assistant—Orange School District*

QUALIFICATIONS

- Associate Degree and Certificate in Business Office Occupations.
- Three years' experience in retail customer service and internship in high school administrative office.
- Excellent word processing skills (examples available); MS Office Suite, including Outlook.
- Bilingual—read, write, and speak fluent Spanish.
- Chosen as leader of college business club.
- Office skills include: 10-key by touch, type 48 WPM.
- Work well with peers on team projects.
- Industrious and dependable—missed only one school day in the last year.
- Quick learner—able to grasp instructions accurately and complete tasks as requested in a timely manner.

EDUCATION

Associate Degree, Business Office Occupations—Administrative Assistant Emphasis

Certificate, Administrative Assistant Program
Fresno City College, Fresno, CA, 2012

- Completed program with a 3.42 GPA
- Officer, Phi Beta Lambda, Student Business Organization

EMPLOYMENT

Internship   **Spring, 2012**
Washington Union High School, Easton, CA

- Completed five-month internship in active administrative office.
- Prepared correspondence and newsletter using MS Word.
- Performed data entry, scheduled appointments, and routed phone messages on multi-line telephone system.
- Translated for Spanish-speaking parents.
- Performed filing tasks—alphabetical and numerical.

Customer Service/Sales Associate (part-time)   **2011–Present**
Bargain Mart, Fresno, CA

- Assist customers with merchandise and ring up sales.
- Stock shelves and price merchandise.
- Received three salary increases while employed at this busy store.
- Offered full-time position upon completing degree.

Figure 1.2 Poor Appearance

Rafael E. Cortez
5559 E. Spruce Ave.
Clovis, CA 93611
(559) 845-9621
rec559@aol.com

OBJECTIVE: Administrative Assistant—Orange School District

QUALIFICATIONS
- Associate Degree and Certificate of Completion in Business Office Occupations.
- Three years' experience in retail customer service and internship in high school administrative office.
- Excellent word processing skills (examples available); MS Office Suite including Outlook.
- Bilingual—read, write, and speak fluent Spanish.
- Chosen as leader of college business club.
- Office skills include: 10-key by touch, type 48 WPM.
- Work well with peers on team projects.
- Industrious and dependable—missed only one school day in the last year.
- Quick learner—able to grasp instructions accurately and complete tasks as requested in a timely manner.

EDUCATION
Associate Degree, Business Office Occupations—Administrative Assistant Emphasis.
Certificate, Administrative Assistant Program.
Fresno City College, Fresno, CA, 2012
Completed program with a 3.42 GPA.
Officer, Phi Beta Lambda, Student Business Organization

EMPLOYMENT
Internship, Spring, 2012
Washington Union High School, Easton, CA
- Completed 5-month internship in active administrative office.
- Prepared correspondence and newsletter using MS Word.
- Assisted in data entry, scheduled appointments, and routed phone messages on multi-line telephone system.
- Translated for Spanish-speaking parents.
- Performed filing tasks—alphabetical and numerical.

Customer Service/Sales Associate (part-time), 2011–Present
Bargain Mart, Fresno, CA
- Assist customers with merchandise and ring up sales.
- Stock shelves and price merchandise.
- Received three salary increases while employed at this busy store.
- Offered full-time position upon completing degree.

Figure 1.3 Four-Year Graduate's Résumé, Customized Format, Marketing Focus

VALERY P. HENDERSON

2942 Marble Drive • San Jose, California 95116
(831) 121-8419 • vhendo@gmail.com

Targeting positions in real estate with firm that will benefit from university business/marketing degree, strong organization skills, and hands-on property management experience.

QUALIFICATIONS

- Substantial property management experience interacting with tenants, collecting rents, assisting with property inspections, preparing payroll, and overseeing maintenance projects.
- Highly dependable with previous job promotions based on reliability, customer service skills, organizational ability, and desire to assume greater responsibility.
- Possess public speaking skills and the ability to communicate effectively with clients. Genuinely enjoy interacting with individuals from diverse backgrounds.
- Organized and detail oriented; accustomed to handling multiple responsibilities simultaneously.
- Computer literate with Microsoft Word, Excel, and PowerPoint.

EDUCATION

Bachelor of Science Degree in Business Administration; Marketing Focus   **2010**
University of San Diego

Highlights
3.62 GPA within major – Dean's List (three semesters)

Affiliations/Activities

- Alumni Chair, Alpha Gamma Rho.
- Initiated alumni relationships through personal contacts and developed new database containing alumni contact information.
- Participated in university-wide fund raising event netting $53K to support Center for Community Solutions. Successfully solicited advertising for event program.
- Assisted in soliciting 10,000 toys for Ronald McDonald House during holiday toy drive.
- Assisted in organizing annual basketball tournament and raising over $80K in two years for St. Mary's Hospital. Also assisted with letter writing campaign for patients at the hospital.

RELEVANT EXPERIENCE

Property Management Assistant   **Summers 2010–2012**
PETALUMA PROPERTIES, Chico, California

- Assisted with management of more than 100 single-family and multi-unit properties. Scope of responsibilities included overseeing maintenance personnel, assigning daily work orders, answering phone inquiries, greeting walk-in clients, collecting rents, preparing payroll, serving 3-day notices, and participating in walk-through property inspections with City inspectors.

ADDITIONAL EMPLOYMENT

Hostess   **Summers 2006–2009**
WONDER VALLEY RESORT, Chico, California

Figure 1.4 Four-Year Graduate's Résumé, Customized Format, Customer Service Focus

ROMAN BALOU

9346 North Martin Avenue
Lodi, California 95240

(209) 831-2654
balou84@yahoo.com

PROFILE

Motivated university graduate with degree in communications desires affiliation with organization that can benefit from four years' experience in retail customer service. Especially competent in settings requiring strong communication, project coordination skills, and an understanding of client-driven organizations. Self-managed and detail-oriented with an effective balance of task and people skills. *Strengths include*:

- Customer Relations
- Project Leadership
- MS Office Suite

- Interpersonal Communication
- Data Research and Analysis
- Ability to Learn New Concepts Quickly

EDUCATION

Bachelor of Arts Degree in Social Science; Communication   2012
Sacramento State University, Sacramento, California

- Member of Village Council—Planned dormitory activities for non-resident students.

EXPERIENCE

- **Customer Service**—Commended by superiors for demonstrating extra effort to assist customers in locating desired information and/or products.
- **New Staff Training**—Trained new hires regarding policies and procedures related to cash handling, register operation, and store closing.
- **Telephone Skills**—Complimented for being well-spoken and helpful when assisting customers with telephone inquiries.
- **Cashiering**—Current evaluations state that cash drawer compliance and balancing was flawless and has resulted in problem-free staff shift changes.
- **Inventory Control**—Experience receiving and checking in new merchandise. Also participated in quarterly inventory reporting.

EMPLOYMENT

Sales Associate   2012–Present
EMPIRE RECORDS, Sacramento, California

Crew Member   2010–2012
TRADER JOE'S, Sacramento, California

Sales Associate – Part-time   2008–2009
BED, BATH, AND BEYOND, Lodi, California

Sales Associate – Part-time   2007–2008
BORDER'S BOOKS, Lodi, California

Identify Your Strengths to Construct a Qualifications Summary and Superior Résumé

Learning Objectives

1. Why is a qualifications summary section so important in the résumé?
2. What is frequently the most important strength to be included in the qualifications summary?
3. Should you list volunteer positions in the qualifications summary and employment section of your résumé?
4. If you do not have reasonably good computer skills, what should you do?

QUALIFICATIONS SUMMARY DEFINED

A qualifications summary is the first *major* section of a résumé. It appears after the heading containing your personal information (name, address, telephone, and e-mail) and the section containing your career objective—the position you want.

For those writing their first résumé, we usually suggest using the heading, Qualifications or Qualifications Summary. However, other frequently used titles for this section include: "Profile," "Professional Summary," "Overview," "Synopsis," and "Management Profile."

The qualifications section highlights your very best credentials. By this we mean it contains your strongest training, skills, and experience in order of importance—your strongest first, then your next strongest, and so on. The qualifications summary section provides an overview or summary of the distinct qualifications you bring to the potential employer. If you do a great job of summarizing your key qualifications in this section, an employer will probably want to read the remainder of the résumé to get more details on your background, and then call you to arrange an interview. If the qualifications you listed are general, abstract, or poorly described, your résumé may be disregarded.

An example of a qualifications summary for an applicant seeking a position working for an electric utility company is provided next.

TOMAS C. RODRIGUEZ
4951 9th Street, Madera, California 93638 • (559) 412-8642 • t.rodrig@sbcglobal.net

---

CAREER FOCUS
ENGINEERING ESTIMATOR, PACIFIC GAS & ELECTRIC

QUALIFICATIONS SUMMARY

EXPERIENCE

- Four years' experience performing electronic repairs, computer operations, utility maintenance, troubleshooting, problem solving, and customer service.
- Trained and practiced in using AutoCAD, DART, and GIS to prepare estimates for construction projects.
- Experienced in reading schematics, flowcharts, GPS devices, and P&IDs.
- Familiar with California Regulations (GO-95, Raptor) relating to utility structures impact on surrounding physical environment.

DEGREES & CERTIFICATES

- Associate of Science Degree, Electrical Systems Technology, *Highest Honors*, 2012.
- Certificate in Building Automation pending—one course required for completion.

PERSONAL ATTRIBUTES

- Proven ability to relate well to peers, supervisors, and professional staff members.
- Noted for punctuality, excellent attendance, and being detail oriented and well organized.
- Enthusiastic, conscientious, and commended for assisting coworkers and department regarding safety and community service programs.
- Consistently pursue additional knowledge and training in electronics and computer hardware and software.

WHAT ARE YOUR STRENGTHS?

Your strengths will usually be found within education and training (including skills acquired), employment, professional achievements and affiliations, honors, awards, military experience, leadership training, languages, computer literacy, and special projects that you have completed. At the end of this chapter you will find an exercise that will help you identify and list your strengths. Be sure to complete the exercise *after* reading the instructions for each category within this chapter; it will make writing your résumé a lot easier—trust us! In Chapter 3 you will take the most significant strengths you have listed for education, training, employment, special projects, honors, organizations, computers, languages, and government service, and concisely place them in the qualifications summary of your résumé.

   Now we are going to focus on each of the sections that are normally included in a résumé. After reading about the type of material to be included in each of these sections, identify and list material from your own personal experience (your strengths) in the area provided in Exercise 2.1 at the end of this chapter.

EDUCATION

In most instances, education and training will be one of your strengths. And for your first résumé, education will probably be your greatest strength. The focus of the education section in your résumé is twofold: 1) to list the degree(s), certificate(s), and honors that you have received during your formal education and 2) to state the specific skills and knowledge you have acquired from the educational program(s) and training that you have completed. Place this material in the designated area on the form in Exercise 2.1 at the end of this chapter.

EMPLOYMENT

No doubt you have worked in either part-time or full-time positions during high school and college. It is essential that you list your employment, even if it was unpaid and not related to the job you are currently seeking. Nearly everyone has worked for someone else—with or without compensation. If this is not the case, immediately go to a teacher, career center, counselor, or mentor and find out how to get some OJT (on-the-job training) in your community. You need to have work experience. The experience may be paid or volunteer. You may work for only a few hours a week, but it is very desirable to gain some experience in a job similar to the one that you eventually want to obtain. Place all your employment experience in the appropriate area on the form in Exercise 2.1.

SPECIAL PROJECTS

Ask yourself if you have completed any of the following at work or school:

1. Initiated a project. Examples: reorganized the stock room; suggested a method to determine how customers initially chose the services of your present employer in order to evaluate advertising effectiveness; suggested a new, time-saving form; or developed a method for notifying patients via e-mail regarding their next appointment—thus substantially reducing postage costs.
2. Developed time-saving methods. Examples: while delivering customer orders, picked up merchandise from suppliers; devised a shortcut to reduce the time it takes to weld a cabinet; or programmed all office phones to autodial the most frequently called suppliers.
3. Taken a leadership role. Examples: became an officer in a student organization; agreed to serve as chairperson for the United Givers Plan at work; or was selected by a teacher to make a presentation to businesses in the community.
4. Saved your employer money. Example: suggested an alternative way to ship merchandise that results in a cost saving.
5. Stood out among your peers. Examples: had the highest sales for a three-month period; assisted a customer who later complimented you in a letter to your employer; or received an earlier-than-expected pay increase.

List any special projects in which you have participated on the Exercise 2.1 form.

HONORS/AWARDS

If your school, peers, employer, or community have honored you—recognized you in some way—it is special and should be included in your résumé. Thus, if you made the Dean's List at your college, graduated in the top 25 percent of your class or program, received a bonus at work, were asked to become a team leader or lead a project, or were designated as employee or student of the month, it is important to an employer and should be noted on your résumé. Place these in the appropriate section of Exercise 2.1.

PROFESSIONAL AND COMMUNITY ORGANIZATIONS

It is important to identify relevant professional and community groups of which you are a member. These can be school or college-affiliated chapters of these organizations. Why are these affiliations important? They show that you are committed to your career choice and desire to become more knowledgeable through membership in, and attendance at, trade or professional meetings. Examples of professional organizations include the American Paralegal Association and the American Student Paralegal Association, Alpha Gamma Sigma, and Phi Beta Lambda. Labor unions sometimes provide education and training for student members. If you have participated in an apprenticeship program, be sure to list it. Being a member of a community organization such as public television, Toastmasters, or the American Heart Association is also positive and should be listed on your résumé. It is even more significant if you have taken an active leadership role, chaired a committee, or served as an officer in a professional or community organization. List any memberships and activities on the Exercise 2.1 form.

COMPUTER LITERACY

Today, everyone needs to be computer literate. Being computer literate means being reasonably well skilled in the use of the Internet for research, e-mail software, and office applications—these are basic to being literate in today's workforce. If you do not have these skills, it is essential that you begin to acquire them immediately.

You should state your computer, Internet, and software skills on your résumé. The operating systems with which you are familiar should be identified. Basically, there are three: Windows 7, Apple/Macintosh, and Linux operating systems. There are some others that are used by computer pros, and if you know how to use them, list them also if you are applying for a position that requires sophisticated computer knowledge. If you are applying for an accounts receivable position, it would be essential to indicate that you have knowledge of bookkeeping/accounting software, such as Excel, Peachtree, Lotus 1-2-3, QuickBooks, etc. The more programs you know, the more valuable you are to an employer. Listing a program does not mean you have to know every aspect of the program. Being familiar with its major functions is sufficient. If you have worked in an office that used customized software for that particular industry, we suggest you list this software as well—it shows you are adaptable and can learn new programs quickly. If you have acquired skills in programming, repairing, networking, assembling, or troubleshooting computers, list these also.

LANGUAGES AND CULTURE

What languages do you speak (besides slang and texting)? For example, if there are significant numbers of Laotians in your community and you speak Lao, it is a plus. Put it on your résumé—it may give you an edge in your job search. In addition to speaking other languages, you may have lived in a country or territory that provided you with special knowledge of the culture or practices within that country. An example would be someone who spent five years living in Mexico working for an airline. If this individual applies for a position with a carrier that has routes to Mexico, it would be beneficial to state that he has knowledge of that country's language, airline industry, and cultural practices.

GOVERNMENT AND MILITARY SERVICE

If you have been a member of the Job, AmeriCorps, or Peace Corps, served in the military, or traveled extensively, you may have acquired skills or knowledge that would be valuable to an employer. Today, many young people have served in the National Guard or performed full-time military service. No doubt training was acquired during their military service that might be transferred to a civilian occupation. Some examples include an EMT (emergency medical technician), or jobs in transportation (dispatcher, driver, forklift operation/repair), and finance (auditor, payroll, accounting).

The key in determining whether to list Job Corps, military, or travel background is whether the knowledge and skills you acquired are *relevant* to the position for which you are applying.

STEPS AFTER COMPLETING EXERCISE 2.1

Congratulations on finishing Exercise 2.1. You have just taken a huge step in completing your résumé. Feel free to go back and add items to the various categories that you listed. You will probably need to return to this form two or three times as you remember most of the relevant items for each category.

Now, we urge you to ask your parents or a brother, sister, or close friend to look at this exercise and see if they fully understand each of the accomplishments and activities you listed. Can they suggest additional items to add to any of these categories? Use their input to expand on the accomplishments you listed.

The final step, if applicable, is to show this exercise to your instructor. He or she may have some additional suggestions.

EXERCISE 2.1

List Your Qualifications

On the lines below place the appropriate answers to the material discussed earlier in this chapter.

a. **Education**

List degrees, certificates, credentials, licenses, and GPA.

_____

_____

_____

_____

_____

b. **Skills**

Indicate skills acquired. Examples: (for a hair stylist) hair styling, coloring, cutting, and sterilization of implements; (for a receptionist) use of multi-line phone system, experience in scheduling appointments, data entry, and greeting customers; and (for an electrician) pulling wire, knowledge of circuitry and electrical controls, reading CAD drawings for initial installations, and VFD applications and installation.

Nearly every occupation and industry has a specific skill set. You can determine the skills that are appropriate by using a college catalog, which contains skill sets taught in each course, or the Dictionary of Occupational Titles, found in most career centers; or by reviewing job descriptions and advertisements. Determine the skills that are appropriate for your occupation and include the most important ones on the résumé.

The following list shows common skills found in office occupations, information technology (IT), and related areas:

Keyboarding/Typing	Office Correspondence	Tax Return Preparation
Statistical Typing	Machine Dictation	Financial Planning
10-Key by Touch	Shorthand/Transcription	Cost Analysis
Bank Reconciliation	Computer Literate	Industrious/Punctual
Bookkeeping	Windows/Macintosh	Team Player
Computer Bookkeeping	Word Processing	Leadership Ability
General Ledger	Programming Languages	Organization Skills
Payroll	Networking Skills	Self-directed
Accounts Payable	Internet Knowledge	Home Page Creation
Accounts Receivable	Software Programs	Work Independently
Auditing	Writing Skills	Problem Solver
Medical Terminology	Foreign Languages	Able to Motivate Others
Legal Terminology	Persuasive People Skills	Decisive/Analytical
Excellent Speller	Dependable/Flexible	Knowledge of Grammar

Now list your skills below:

_____

_____

_____

_____

_____

_____

_____

_____

c. **Employment.**

List employers (paid or volunteer) with *most recent first*. State the following information:

1. Employer's business name (accurately spelled) as found online or in the telephone book
2. Dates of employment—beginning and ending

3. Your job title

4. What you did and the skills used or acquired on the job

5. Training received and any training provided to other employees

6. Promotions received—state job titles from initial position to final/current position

7. Responsibilities—for example, opening/closing store, making bank deposits, authorizing overtime, buying new equipment, etc.

8. Major accomplishments/achievements—examples would be completing a 12-week training program in 9 weeks, or having the fewest customer complaints of anyone in the office over a three-year period

9. Evaluations—comments (written statements about your performance) and/or ratings (sometimes stated as numbers or as "good, excellent, superior") on formal evaluations

_____

_____

_____

_____

_____

_____

_____

_____

_____

_____

_____

_____

d. Special Projects.

Refer to the material described earlier in the chapter for information on what to place in this area.

_____

_____

_____

_____

_____

_____

e. Honors or Awards.

State the honors and awards you have received at school, work, in the community, or in the military. These can be for attendance, sports, tutoring other students—any type of recognition.

_____

_____

_____

_____

_____

f. Professional and Community Organizations.

List the professional (work-related), community, and school-related organizations of which you are or have been a member. Also list any offices held, projects completed for these organizations, or special recognition or awards you received.

_____

_____

_____

_____

g. Computer Literacy.

Indicate the following:

1. Type of computer systems you have operated (Windows, Apple, or Linux)

2. Software programs that you can use

3. Programming skills

4. Hardware skills—can you repair or upgrade a computer?

5. Networking knowledge

6. Internet and e-mail skills

7. Social media skills (LinkedIn, Twitter, Facebook, blogs, etc.)

_____

_____

_____

_____

_____

_____

h. Languages.

Indicate any language with which you are familiar. State your level of skill (conversational, studied two years, fluent) and whether you can read, write, understand, and/or speak the language.

_____

_____

_____

_____

i. Government and Military Service.

State the type of government service that you have performed—paid or volunteer is okay. You may have already listed this under employment. If not, state it here and provide the same information as you would for a job. Be sure to list government and military skills/training in civilian terms or words, not military or government jargon.

_____

_____

_____

_____

CHAPTER 3

Developing the Key Sections of Your Résumé

Learning Objectives

1. Why should a résumé clearly state a specific job or type of position as its focus?
2. What is a power statement, and where should it appear on your résumé?
3. Why is the qualifications summary considered to be the heart of your résumé?
4. Which should take top billing in the qualifications summary, your experience or your education?

RÉSUMÉ FORMAT

The résumé format described in this chapter is suggested for your first résumé. This is the same format that was used in the sample résumé, Figure 1.1 (Chapter 1).

The first section in a résumé is the *heading: it contains your name, address, telephone number(s), and e-mail address.* Center these lines at the top of the page, beginning one inch below the top edge of the paper, as shown in the following example:

MELVIN H. MURGATROY
1479 South Ocean Blvd.
Hollywood, CA 90019
(416) 897-2828
lcapitan@titanicuniversity.edu

Next, you will place the word *objective* **or** *focus* in bold capitals at the left margin.

OBJECTIVE/FOCUS

Then,

QUALIFICATIONS SUMMARY

and the remaining sections as follows:

EDUCATION

SKILLS

EMPLOYMENT

ORGANIZATIONS & ACTIVITIES

Now that you have an overview of the section headings that will appear on your résumé, we will examine each of the sections individually, provide examples, and discuss what goes in each section and why.

OBJECTIVE/FOCUS/POWER STATEMENT

We like the words *objective* and *focus* equally well, and use them interchangeably on résumés. It is wise to have a *specific* job in mind for placement in the objective section. Employers emphatically believe you should know the type of position that you are seeking, think you would enjoy, and for which you have developed skill sets. Employers believe that if you do not know the type of work that you want to do, you may be with them only a short time until something else catches your imagination. Employers recruit potential employees hoping that they will stay with them for a long time, as it is costly and time-consuming to train new employees.

An example of the objective section for one who is seeking a position as a receptionist:

OBJECTIVE *RECEPTIONIST POSITION*

We recommend that most beginning job hunters state a specific job or general position for which they have been trained. You will have much better results if you state an objective. Often you will simply state the title of the position that has been advertised, listed on a job description, or passed on to you by someone in the company to which you are applying. But the position should be one for which you are qualified.

You will note that when you state your objective/focus, it should be placed three spaces below the address and appear in bold and/or capital letters to bring the reader's attention to it easily.

You can enhance your objective/focus statement with what is termed a "power statement." A power statement indicates the position you desire and also states your most outstanding qualifications, for example:

FOCUS *RECEPTIONIST—EXPERIENCED AND TRAINED IN MULTI-LINE PHONE SYSTEMS, CUSTOMER SERVICE, HUMAN RELATIONS, AND DATA ENTRY*

Perhaps it is obvious why this is called a power statement, as one can easily and immediately determine that the applicant has excellent skills in greeting customers, answering telephones, and data entry. Thus, by mentioning these strong skills in the objective/focus statement, it gets the reader/employer's attention and makes an immediate impact. You may recall that employers spend only a short time scanning résumés unless they see something that grabs their interest. The purpose of the power statement is to get their attention immediately so they will want to look at the remainder of the résumé and then give you a call to see if you are as good in person as you appear to be in the résumé.

If you want your résumé to focus on a broader range of jobs, another option would be to omit the objective/focus section. Usually this is not recommended because it may appear that you do not have a career direction. However, if you are applying to a company that has several positions for which you believe you are qualified, you may not want to specify only one position. To continue with the example in the focus/power statement for the receptionist above, let us assume that you were submitting a résumé to a company that had positions open for a receptionist, administrative assistant, marketing assistant, and payroll clerk. If you submit a résumé with an objective/focus for the receptionist position, and the company has many well-qualified candidates and fills that position with someone other than you, they probably would not consider you for the other three positions. However, if your résumé contains skills that might qualify you for all four positions, it would be smart to *not* state a specific job. Our recommendation would be to omit the objective/focus portion or make it more inclusive so that you will appear qualified for all four positions.

QUALIFICATIONS SUMMARY

The qualifications summary is the heart of a well-written résumé and contains an overview of your major qualifications. In this section, your best qualifications are to be stated simply and concisely. To do this, you will need to refer to Figure 1.1 (Chapter 1) and Exercise 2.1 (Chapter 2). We suggest that you remove the pages containing Figure 1.1 and Exercise 2.1, and then place them in front of you as you complete the remainder of the sections in your résumé.

In this section you are to take your *best* qualifications in education, training, employment, special projects, honors, organizations, computers, languages, and government service and then concisely list them in the qualifications portion of your résumé. This step can be easily accomplished, and it is critical to preparing a winning résumé. If there were *key words* (specific words stating desired skills, for example: Excel spreadsheet development, 10-key by touch, customer relations) in the job announcement, it is essential that you use these key words to describe your qualifications—assuming you have these skills. Only include your most outstanding achievements regarding education, employment, skills, and so on, in the qualifications summary.

A central idea to remember while you complete your résumé and the qualifications section is that the most relevant/important information related to the position for which you are applying should appear *first*. Follow this guideline throughout the construction of your résumé. In addition to putting the most relevant material first, place the most *recent* experiences *first*.

In the qualifications section of Figure 1.1 (the résumé for Rafael Cortez), you will note that the first item listed is an "Associate Degree in Business Office Occupations." This is probably the single most important qualification relating to his seeking an administrative assistant's position. Note that information regarding his degree is more fully detailed under the education section.

The next item in Rafael Cortez's qualifications section states, "Three years' experience in retail customer service and internship in high school administrative office." This refers to his three years of experience as a Customer Service/Sales Associate at Bargain Mart and his internship at Washington Union High School—both are listed with more information under the employment section. However, inclusion in the qualifications' section is important for several reasons:

- It shows he held one job for several years.
- It indicates that he has interacted successfully with customers and peers.
- He probably acquired some training in customer service, which will be useful to future employers.
- He has actual experience working in the administrative offices of a school.

The same concepts apply to the other items contained in the qualifications section. Many other items appearing in the qualifications section are also listed elsewhere on the résumé in more detail. Sometimes statements regarding accomplishments or characteristics that appear in the qualifications section do not have more detail in other locations on the résumé. An example from the Cortez résumé is the statement, "Industrious and dependable—missed only one school day in the last year." This statement appears only in the qualifications section of the résumé as no additional details are necessary. In essence the statement is complete and speaks for itself.

The following are examples of résumé qualifications sections for an IT technician and a food service worker (cook in training).

QUALIFICATIONS

- Associate of Science Degree and Certificate of Achievement in Networking/Computer Technician Program.
- Experience troubleshooting computer systems and providing support to institutional and corporate clients.
- Comprehensive knowledge of Microsoft networking and software systems, servers, workstations, and PC hardware components.
- Trained in installations relating to broadband: DSL, Cable, Satellite, and T-1.
- Software applications include: Windows NT Server and Workstations, Win 7, XP, DOS 6.X; Linux; MS Office Suite, FrontPage, Publisher, and Internet Explorer; Corel Office Suite; and Adobe Acrobat.

QUALIFICATIONS

- Associate Degree in Food and Nutrition.
- Two years of experience as Prep Cook with local restaurants; received "Employee of the Month" award, January, 2012.
- Trained in meat cutting, baking, use of seasonings, salad preparation, food and beverage purchasing, and food sanitation.
- Additional part-time experience (2 years) as retail sales clerk.
- Bilingual: read, write, and speak fluent Spanish.
- Learn quickly and relate well to coworkers and management.

Now it is your turn. In completing Exercise 3.1, place the pages containing the answers to Exercise 2.1, Chapter 2, in front of you and select your most significant qualifications related to the position you are applying for, and then place them in Exercise 3.1 on the next page.

EXERCISE 3.1

QUALIFICATIONS

1. _____
   _____
   _____

2. _____
   _____
   _____

3. _____
   _____
   _____

4. _____
   _____
   _____

5. _____
   _____
   _____

6. _____
   _____
   _____

7. _____
   _____
   _____

8. _____
   _____
   _____

9. _____
   _____
   _____

EDUCATION

If you have just completed an educational program and have limited related employment experience, the next section will typically consist of your educational background. However, if you have substantial employment or related experience, the employment section would appear next. Again, the principle is to put the *most important* (important in qualifying you for the job you are seeking) *sections closest to the beginning of the résumé.*

Should you indicate that you have received a high school diploma in the education section? The answer is usually "no" if you received a degree or certificate beyond high school or if you have substantial work experience in the field in which you are applying. Generally, your high school coursework and projects are preparatory for your obtaining further, more specialized training in college, a vocational school, or on the job. Of course there are exceptions. If you have noteworthy achievements in high school such as being elected student body president or named a National Merit scholar, or if you received some prestigious state or national award, we suggest that you include this under education or the qualifications summary. This caliber of recognition will set you apart from your peers. However, this material should only be included when you are seeking your first employment opportunity. After you have finished your schooling and been employed for two years, we suggest you no longer include high school accomplishments.

In the education section of the résumé, state your education in the following order:

1. The degree, certificate, or program you completed, and your major course or field of study
2. The college you attended and its location
3. The date the program was or will be completed
4. Your class ranking and/or GPA (grade point average), if above a 3.0 ("B" average)
5. Any special awards, honors, or recognition

An example of the education section for a Legal Office Administrative (secretary) major would be as follows:

EDUCATION   **Associate in Applied Science Degree, Legal Office Administration**
Heald College, San Francisco, CA, 2012
Graduated in top 10% of class
GPA: 3.82 within major
Recipient: "Outstanding Legal Office Administration Graduate Award"

Special Skills

Sometimes a special skills section is inserted after the education section and before the employment section. This would be the case if the legal office administration applicant mentioned earlier had special skills in law office administration that were not mentioned elsewhere.

For example:

LEGAL OFFICE SKILLS   *Competencies include:*
Software: WordPerfect Office X5, legal mode
MS Word
FastTrack Schedule 10
VerdictSearch
Calendaring
Billing
Filing
Table of Authorities
Tickler files

If you have a special skills section like this one, it would normally be placed after the education section. Also, you might take the most significant parts of the skills section and place them in the qualifications section at the very top of the résumé, such as:

- Excellent legal word processing skills using WordPerfect Legal and FastTrack.

Professional Licenses and Certifications

Those who have received professional licenses or certifications from a state agency should indicate this in their résumés. Sometimes a certification is received from a professional association or manufacturer (Microsoft is an example); this is significant because it communicates to an employer that this applicant has passed a difficult testing program and received recognition as a certified specialist. Certification or licensing by a state or national organization or agency is a strong selling point to a prospective employer. So if you have it, be sure to put it on your résumé. Place it under education or skills, unless you really want to bring attention to it. Then it is best to have a separate heading that will really spotlight it (see the example in next paragraph).

The following licenses and certifications are listed for a dental back office applicant:

LICENSE & CERTIFICATIONS

- Idaho X-Ray License, issued January, 2011.
- Coronal Polish Certificate.
- Certified in Spanish Language, Intermediate Level Examination, 2012.

EMPLOYMENT

In most résumés for recent graduates, the employment section will appear next. This section is sometimes referred to as the "Experience" or "Employment History" section.

The items in an employment listing include the following:

1. Job title—if it is part-time, say so—then state dates of employment (usually at the far right so that they can be viewed easily).
2. Employer's name (use the firm's business name, not the manager or your supervisor's name), city, and state.
3. Your responsibilities and achievements with this employer. Some key things prospective employers look for in this section are the following:
   A. Whether you have long-term and continuous employment, as opposed to many jobs lasting only one, two, or three months.
   B. Time gaps between employment (unaccounted for time periods between employers create questions in a prospective employer's mind).

The following example is an employment section for someone seeking back office medical assisting employment.

EMPLOYMENT

Medical Assistant Internship – Back Office   Fall, 2011
Kenneth Yogata, M.D., Peoria, Illinois

- Assisted with minor surgery, patient examinations, and instructed patients regarding physical therapy.
- Additional activities included recording patient's symptoms, medical history, and blood pressure; sanitizing examination rooms; and preparing trays for subsequent procedures.
- Offered part-time paid position upon the completion of internship program.

MISCELLANEOUS RÉSUMÉ SECTIONS

Additional sections such as participation in professional and community organizations or service in the military or Peace Corps may be included in a résumé if these are part of your background, and the skills acquired are relevant to the position you are seeking. The following sections describe when and how to integrate this type of material into your résumé. References are discussed in Chapter 8.

Organizations and Activities

Those who are active in professional and community organizations tend to be people-oriented—meaning they usually relate well to other people. Getting along with people may be the most important skill you possess. We all know individuals who are very talented and quite bright but have difficulty interacting with their peers, bosses, or customers. Substantial research indicates that *more employees lose their jobs due to poor human relations skills than for any other reason*. Employers want to know if you have been involved in social and professional groups because they believe this will make you a better team player.

There is another reason that employers react positively to your belonging to *professional* groups. Membership in professional groups often provides opportunities for increased technical knowledge, networking/leadership opportunities, and professional growth. In a nutshell, what this really means is that someone who is professionally active will be better informed regarding what is happening in their occupation/industry. He or she will probably receive a publication, attend professional meetings where workshops regarding the latest concepts and technology are discussed, and will regularly meet people at conferences who are excited and knowledgeable about this occupation and industry.

The following is an example of an organizations and activities section for a management trainee applicant seeking a job with a major fast food chain.

ORGANIZATIONS/ACTIVITIES

- Member/Treasurer, Students in Free Enterprise (SIFE).
- Member of SIFE college team that placed first in state competition, third in international competition, Kansas City, MO, 2012.
- Cheerleader 2 years; Head Cheerleader 1 year.
- Member, Fellowship of Christian Athletes.

Military, Job/Peace Corps/AmeriCorps

Military service is usually listed under either employment or education if you acquired substantial training while serving in the military. The same would be true for the Job or Peace Corps. Place all the relevant experience, education, and skills that you have acquired under those sections.

References

References should be placed on a separate sheet. An example of the suggested format is provided in Chapter 8, which also discusses the appropriate format for a salary history and when it is appropriate to include information regarding previous earnings.

CHAPTER 4

Essentials and Examples in Résumé Presentation

Learning Objectives

1. What is "white space," and why is it important on your résumé?
2. What percentage of résumés for new college graduates should be one page in length?
3. Identify some of the qualities that are necessary to give your résumé an attractive appearance.
4. What is considered to be "fluff" in a résumé? Why is it discouraged?

ATTRACTIVE APPEARANCE AND FORMAT

If you were going to sell your car, what would you do first? Would you make the car look as good as possible by washing and detailing it? Probably so! Well, the same principle applies to selling yourself and your talents. Your résumé is designed to market you to a prospective employer, resulting in your being called for an interview. You can do this by presenting a résumé that is professional in appearance. It is not difficult to do this in an age of word processors and laser printers. With very little effort, you can take advantage of the features available in the major word processing programs—MS Word and WordPerfect—to look professional on paper. If you do not have a personal computer or laptop at home, try your public library or the computer lab at the community college.

In addition to preparing your résumé on a word processor, it is suggested that you prepare digital copies of your résumé using Adobe (PDF) and ASCII (plain text) formatting. A discussion of why this may be important to you and how to do this will be included in Chapter 5.

The major software programs have features that will assist you to:

- Automatically center text horizontally and vertically (use the block or select copy feature and then use the centering feature).
- Place text in *italics*, **bold**, or <u>underline</u> (use the block or select copy feature and then the text formatting feature).
- Use bullets (like those that appear at the left margin) or symbol and Wingding font sets (→, ■, ♦) to emphasize and bring attention to important material on your résumé.
- Place material (such as dates of employment) adjacent to the right margin—known as the "flush right" or "align right" feature.
- Use a horizontal line to separate sections of the résumé—in the first résumé example, the address is separated from the objective by two horizontal lines (Figure 1.1, Chapter 1).

Using these features adds greatly to the attractiveness of your résumé; so does the absence of spelling and grammatical errors (see the "Error-Free" section in this chapter). Both major software programs offer features which check the spelling of *most* words, but not all—remember company and individual names will not be checked. Nor will spell check features correct words that sound nearly the same as the intended word, but are not spelled incorrectly, e.g., typing "manger" when the intended word is "manager," or typing "for" when you intend "four." This is another reason to have a human proofreader as well. These programs also have tools that help correct punctuation and grammatical errors. Use them; they will pay big dividends.

Although the major word processing programs offer résumé templates that can be utilized to prepare a résumé, the authors do not recommend their use. The reasons are that they prevent you from personalizing and customizing your résumé; they are easily recognized as templates and demonstrate little in the way of originality and word processing skills, and are difficult to change or alter unless your résumé fits the "cookie cutter" formats that the software makers envisioned.

Another way to make your résumé more attractive is to use substantial "white space." This term means to leave white or blank areas before and after printed text. You may have seen a full-page advertisement in a magazine or newspaper where the company has placed only *one word* on the page. Everyone who looks at that page will be drawn to the one word—which is usually a company or product name. White space around text causes the reader to focus on the text. The more white space you place around a section of your résumé, the more likely it will grab the reader's attention.

The following examples, taken from the qualifications section in Figure 1.1, Chapter 1, illustrate this concept. In the first example below, please note how the applicant's achievements stand out when substantial white space is placed before and after each of the bulleted items. Then compare it to the second example where there is a minimum of white space between the bulleted paragraphs. Very little seems to stand out in the second example—the material tends to run together.

QUALIFICATIONS

- Associate Degree and Certificate of Completion in Business Office Occupations.

- Three years' experience in retail customer service and internship in high school administrative office.

- Excellent word processing skills (examples available); MS Office Suite, including Outlook.

- Bilingual—read, write, and speak fluent Spanish.

- Chosen as leader of college business club.

- Office skills include: 10-key by touch, type 48 WPM, and work well with peers on team projects.

- Industrious and dependable—missed only one school day in the last year.

- Quick learner—able to grasp instructions accurately and complete tasks as requested in a timely manner.

QUALIFICATIONS

- Associate Degree and Certificate of Completion in Business Office Occupations.
- Three years' experience in retail customer service and internship in high school administrative office.
- Excellent word processing skills (examples available); MS Office Suite, including Outlook.
- Bilingual—read, write, and speak fluent Spanish.
- Chosen as leader of college business club.
- Office skills include: 10-key by touch, type 48 WPM, and work well with peers on team projects.
- Industrious and dependable—missed only one school day in the last year.
- Quick learner—able to grasp instructions accurately and complete tasks as requested in a timely manner.

WELL ORGANIZED

How should you organize the material on your résumé? We think you can already answer that question—*the most important information related to the position you are seeking appears at the top of the page*. Ninety-nine percent of the readers of this book should have résumés that are *one page* in length. You will recall that the sections of a résumé are normally as follows:

- HEADING (your name, address, and so on centered one inch from top of page)
- OBJECTIVE/FOCUS (on third line below last line of heading, and usually at left)
- QUALIFICATIONS SUMMARY
- EDUCATION (sometimes education and employment appear in reverse order)
- SKILLS (if applicable to your résumé)
- LICENSE/S & CERTIFICATION/S (if applicable)
- EMPLOYMENT
- ORGANIZATIONS/ACTIVITIES (if applicable)

This format is typical and considered to be professionally appropriate. However, there are many variations of this format. You will see an example at the end of this chapter and several examples in Appendix A that, although very similar to the format above, have a slightly different appearance. They illustrate how the appearance and content of a résumé may vary after you have a number of years of experience. You may also become creative in your layout or have a certified résumé writer help you prepare your résumé. For now, the format presented in this text will serve you well. Your biggest challenge will be to write it with a high degree of professionalism. Do it well, and you will receive more than your share of interviews.

WORD PROCESSED AND LASER/INK JET PRINTED

By using a word processor and saving to disk (saving a copy to your hard drive, a memory stick, or a CD), you will have a permanent copy of your résumé to:

- modify for a specific position.
- change and add to in the future as your experience/training accumulates.
- retrieve from the computer and, using the tools available on most word processors, quickly make your résumé and accompanying materials contemporary in appearance.

When submitting printed copies of your résumé, it is strongly suggested that you use a laser or ink jet printer to provide print quality that has a professional look. If you do not have this kind of a printer at home, copy your résumé onto a memory stick or CD and have your local copy store print it using a laser printer.

ERROR-FREE

Your résumé should contain *no spelling, typographical, grammatical, or punctuation errors*! You can avoid errors in your résumé by using the tools in the word processing program, having several knowledgeable friends and teachers look it over, and asking a potential employer to review it and make suggestions for improvement. When you ask a prospective employer to review your résumé, you are asking for help without putting any pressure on him or her for a job. This a good way to network with likely employers without making demands on them. Good writing comes from rewriting many times. Write it, sleep on it, and then rewrite it again and again. It takes time, but the result will be well worth it.

Remember, employers use résumés to assess job candidates' qualifications, but they also use them to *screen out* those whom they think will not make good employees. One way they do this is to eliminate candidates who make spelling, typographical, grammatical, and punctuation errors in their application materials. Notice the words "application materials." You can prepare a great résumé, but if you make a glaring spelling mistake in the cover letter, employment application, or other preliminary employment documents, it becomes a negative factor.

BRIEF—ONE PAGE

Yes, keep it short. We write résumés daily for professional people with 0 to 35 years of experience and the majority of these résumés are one page in length, occasionally two, and sometimes more for senior executives or academics with advanced degrees. If professional people with this much experience can get the essentials down to one page, we are sure that most readers of this résumé guide can do the same.

Employers are busy, often reviewing 30, 40, or 100 résumés for an open position. When they receive large numbers of résumés, they spend only a very short time looking at a candidate's qualifications. Thus, if you have your best "stuff" in the qualifications section of your résumé, and it appears near the top on a one-page résumé, it stands the best chance of being noticed.

SPECIFIC STATEMENTS REGARDING ACCOMPLISHMENTS/SKILLS

Do you know what the word "fluff" means? A résumé with fluff contains a lot of generalizations, but very few specifics. Employers want to see *specific accomplishments or skills* stated in the résumé. The following are examples of the "right way" and the "wrong way" to list accomplishments in the qualifications section of a résumé:

RIGHT WAY	WRONG WAY
• Graduated 7th in a class of 60, and was named "Outstanding Interior Design Student" in 2009.	• Received many honors during my college program.
• Knowledgeable regarding air conditioning/heating installation, maintenance, troubleshooting, controls, ducting, and systems balancing.	• Possess substantial skills regarding air conditioning and heating equipment.
• Experience using Windows 7 & XP, Excel, Quick Books, WordPerfect, and Famous Bookkeeping software.	• Am familiar with most types of PCs and software.
• Completed 6 years of formal Spanish training—speak, read, and write fluently.	• Bilingual—speak Spanish.
• Excellent communications and human relations skills—completed Dale Carnegie course in 2009 and was named Employee of the Month in December.	• Get along well with staff at work.

STYLE

Style refers to the way you write or present your qualifications in your résumé and other marketing documents that you prepare. You will note in the examples of résumés that appear later in this chapter that all are one page in length. They are written with brevity to maximize "punch." In other words, they are written to show your strengths in the least amount of space, utilizing *action-oriented* words—words indicating achievement or active participation in projects in work-related activities.

How can you write with punch? First, use the first person ("I"), but only assume or imply the pronoun "I" in your statements regarding your qualifications, employment, and so on; you do not actually write or include "I" in the statement. An example from Rafael Cortez's résumé appearing in Figure 1.1, Chapter 1, states, "Associate Degree and Certificate of Completion in Business Office Occupations." What is assumed or implied in the qualifications statement is that Cortez has an associate degree and certificate in Business Office Occupations. Because the style for résumés should be *brief* and written in *first person*, rather than say, "I have an Associate Degree and Certificate in Business Office Occupations," the writer simply implies the "I have an" portion of the sentence. Thus, write only, *Associate Degree and Certificate of Completion in Business Office Occupations.* This style of writing takes a little practice but is not difficult.

Action words are verbs that communicate *positive acts* (action) and achievement on your part. In Rafael Cortez's résumé (Figure 1.1 in Chapter 1), the following was written in the employment section:

- Completed five-month internship in busy administrative office.
- Prepared correspondence and newsletter using MS Word.
- Assisted in data entry, scheduling appointments, and routing phone messages on multi-line telephone system.
- Translated for Spanish-speaking parents.
- Performed filing tasks—alphabetically and numerically.

Note that all of the bulleted items begin with "action words," or the verbs *completed*, *prepared*, *assisted*, *translated*, and *performed*. These words show positive action taken and achievement by the writer. Here are additional action words that can be used in résumés and cover letters:

achieved	*earned*	*initiated*
increased	*improved*	*planned*
originated	*reduced*	*trained*
organized	*presented*	*evaluated*
produced	*arranged*	*created*
customized	*implemented*	*designed*
installed	*built*	*promoted*

Omitting articles is also essential in good résumé writing. Articles include *the, a,* and *an.* By omitting them, you will keep your résumé brief and to the point. Note the following example from Cortez's employment section, previously shown, which contains no articles.

- Completed five-month internship in active administrative office.

In normal writing style, we would write a sentence as follows: *I* completed *a* five-month internship in *an* active administrative office. But to give it punch and keep it brief, the "I," "a," and "an" were omitted.

SAMPLE RÉSUMÉS—EISCHEN'S SIMPLIFIED FORMAT

The examples (Figures 4.1 through 4.7) of résumés for career-entry applicants that follow are intended as illustrations of the simplified résumé format discussed earlier. Check these sample résumés for the key components of a résumé: *attractive, well organized, word processed, laser/ink-jet printed, error-free, one page in length,* and *specific regarding accomplishments/skills.*

Example 4.8 illustrates a more complex format used in a four-year graduate's résumé.

Figure 4.1 System Network Technician

HENRY YEE

1214 E. Oleander Ave ◆ Sacramento, CA 94230
(916) 845-3626 ◆ hyee@yahoo.com

FOCUS *SYSTEM NETWORK TECHNICIAN*

QUALIFICATIONS

- Associate in Applied Science Degree in Microsoft and Cisco Networking Technology.
- Earned Network+ and A+ Certified Technician status.
- Hands-on experience troubleshooting and repairing computers in office with 800 nodes.
- Knowledgeable regarding MS NT, Win 7, Vista, XP, 2000, and DOS operating systems.
- Proficient in configuring and troubleshooting computer hardware: desktop and laptop units, routers, servers, and workstations.
- Able to effectively communicate with non-technical staff members regarding IT issues.
- Software program knowledge includes: MS Office, Publisher, Visual Basic, Visio, and Cakewalk.
- Achievements: 100% Attendance Award, Dean's List Award, and earned 3.97 GPA.

EDUCATION

Associate Degree in Applied Science, Microsoft and Cisco Networking Technology
Heald College, Sacramento, CA,   **2012**
GPA: 3.9

SKILLS

- Experience with computer installations, configuration, and management of servers, workstations, routers, switches, domains, and networks of various sizes.
- Ability to diagnose and resolve connectivity and configuration conflicts with peripherals and other computer hardware devices.
- Modify workstation clients and printers to connect via network while configuring TCP/IP, IP Address, Default Gateway, and DNS settings.

EXPERIENCE

Technology Internship **(360 Hours)**
McClatchy High School, Sacramento, CA   **2011**

- Diagnosed and resolved computer/network related problems in large network system with 800 stations.
- Installed and configured operating systems and numerous applications, for example, GroupWise, PowerSchool, Norton Ghost, and Deep Freeze.

Figure 4.2 Medical Assistant—Front Office

MADELINE M. MOSCONI

8712 E. Peach Ave ♦ Chowchilla, CA 93612

(559) 298-3626 ♦ mmm1412@yahoo.com

FOCUS: *MEDICAL ASSISTANT – FRONT or BACK OFFICE*

QUALIFICATIONS

- Associate Degree in Applied Science, Medical Assisting.
- Software applications and familiarity: Medical Manager, Microsoft Word, Excel, Power-Point, and Access.
- Externship experience included: scheduling appointments, greeting patients and placing in examination room, taking vitals and recording data in patient's chart, filing, and cashiering.
- Familiar with medical records, terminology, and anatomy.
- Clinical procedures training and experience includes: taking vital signs, suture removal, urinalysis, and administering oral vaccines.
- Office skills include: Keyboarding, 44 WPM; hands-on training in billing, collections, bookkeeping, and use of multi-line phone systems.
- Well practiced people skills with ability to relate to patients of various cultures and languages.

EDUCATION

Associate Degree in Applied Science - Medical Assisting
San Joaquin College, Fresno, CA   **2012**
GPA: 3.82

CLINICAL SKILLS

- Phlebotomy, Pharmacology, EKG Documentation, and Clinical and Laboratory procedures.
- Coding, ICD 9 and CPT, Medical Transcription and Terminology.
- Hematology (CBC – Cholestech and Glucose).

EXPERIENCE

Medical Assistant Externship (160 Hours)
Chowchilla Medical Center, Chowchilla, CA   **2011**

- Scheduled appointments, filed patient charts, answered multi-line phone system, made notations on charts, set up examination rooms, stocked pharmacy sample room, completed lab forms, recorded flu vaccinations, and called in prescriptions.

Cashier
Beacon Mini-Mart, Madera, CA   **2010–2011**

- Received payments/made change for gasoline and merchandise, processed credit card transactions, reconciled cash drawer, prepared deposits, stocked shelves, and cleaned store.

Figure 4.3 Marketing Assistant

RAMONA E. BROOKS
1218 E. Montecito, Apt. 19
Fresno, CA 93707
(559) 225-0404 – reb500@hotmail.com

OBJECTIVE

MARKETING ASSISTANT POSITION

QUALIFICATIONS

- Associate Degree in Business Administration, Marketing emphasis.
- Three years of customer service experience in retail settings.
- Experience planning and implementing special promotions, including flyers, advertising copy, and special displays for major retailer's cosmetics department.
- Software skills: Dreamweaver, Corel Presentations, and MS FrontPage, PowerPoint, Word, and Excel; keyboarding speed: 60+ WPM.
- Creative in use of graphics and drawing—freehand and with custom computer software.
- Excellent problem-solving skills and ability to work well under pressure.
- Interact well with coworkers and management—completed courses in human relations, communications, and supervision.

EMPLOYMENT

Cosmetics Counter Manager   2011–Present
J. C. PENNEY, Fresno, CA

- Earned "All Star" award for consistently meeting or exceeding monthly and yearly quotas.
- Plan and develop special promotions including flyers, advertising copy, and special displays.
- Process orders, product returns, and resolve customer service concerns.

Payroll Assistant   2009–2011
TWELFTH STREET COURIER SERVICE, Everett, Mississippi

- Utilized computer accounting system to prepare payroll, accounts payable/receivable, and payroll taxes. Prepared bank deposits and reconciled bank accounts.

EDUCATION

Associate of Arts Degree in Business Administration 2012
Fresno City College, Fresno, CA

- Maintained 3.2 GPA while working full-time.
- Earned 100% of living and education expenses while completing degree.

    Activities: Alpha Gamma Sigma (Fresno City College Honor Society)
                  Treasurer, Students in Free Enterprise (SIFE)
                  Volunteer, Ronald McDonald House

Figure 4.4 Dental Hygienist

KRISTEN A. KHAM, RDH

9619 N. Pineapple Way   (408) 299-1798
San Francisco, CA 93786   kakham@sfusanfran.edu

FOCUS

*CAREER DENTAL HYGIENIST POSITION REQUIRING DEDICATION TO
PREVENTIVE DENTISTRY, STRONG INTERPERSONAL SKILLS,
AND DENTAL PRACTICE EXPERIENCE*

QUALIFICATIONS

- Associate of Science Degree in Dental Hygiene.
- Licenses and certification for local anesthesia, radiation, curettage, dental assisting, and CPR.
- Dental hygiene experience (more than 1,000 hours) in clinical setting where complete prophylaxis and patient care services were provided.
- Prior experience as Back Office Dental Assistant—assisted in general dentistry practice preparing setup and break down of operatories, cements, crown preparation. Also provided information regarding post-operative care.
- Commended for demonstrating initiative in back office duties; subsequently received year-end bonus.
- Excellent human relations/people skills—completed communications and team-building seminar for enhancing relationships with patients and peers.

EDUCATION

Associate of Science Degree, Dental Hygiene   2012
San Francisco City College
San Francisco, California
Honors:
  Dean's Medallion Award (placed in top 10% of graduating class).
  Dean's List: 3.81 GPA on 4.0 scale.

EMPLOYMENT

Dental Hygiene Clinical Practice, 1,000 Hours   2012
San Francisco City College Dental Hygiene Clinic
San Francisco, California

Dental Assistant, Back Office (part-time)   2009–2011
Harold P. Martin, DDS
- Assisted with general dentistry procedures: extractions, crown preparation, setup and break down of operatories, patient postoperative care, and patient education.

PROFESSIONAL LICENSES/CERTIFICATES/AFFILIATIONS

California Board of Dental
  Hygiene License
Dental Radiology License
Dental Assisting and CPR
  Certificates

Local Anesthesia, Nitrous Oxide &
  Curettage Certified
American/California Dental Hygienists'
  Association
Bay Area Dental Hygienists' Association

Figure 4.5 Brake/Front End Specialist

LOLO E. CONTRERAS
4545 W. Martin Luther Blvd.
Selma, CA 93786
(559) 297-7274
leccontr@jahoo.com

OBJECTIVE

BRAKE/FRONT END SPECIALIST—CAREER POSITION

QUALIFICATIONS

- Brakes, Suspension, and Steering Certificate, 2012.
- Completed 600 hours of hands-on training in:
  Alignment (Thrustline & Total Four-Wheel)
  Power Drum and Disc Brakes, plus introduction to ABS theory
  Suspension and Steering Repair, CV Boot/Joint Service, and Axle Maintenance
- Received instruction regarding precision measurement, fasteners, gaskets, tubing, wiring, friction and anti-friction bearings, work orders, and cost/job estimating.
- Equipment used in training included:
  Hunter J-111
  Computerized off-the-car balancers
  On-the-car balancers
  AMMCO Drum and Rotor Lathe
  Specialty tools and hydraulic presses

EDUCATION

Certificate of Completion, Brakes, Suspension, and Steering   **2012**
Vocational Training Center, Fresno City College
Fresno, California
- Completed certificate program four weeks ahead of schedule.
- Received instructor's recommendation upon completion of program.

EMPLOYMENT

Brake Service Specialist (Part-time)   **4/2011–Present**
Elmer's Superior Brake Service
Fowler, California
- Employed weekends and evenings while completing brake and suspension training.
- Began at minimum wage and received two hourly wage increases.
- Work includes servicing brakes and suspension systems on commercial vehicles and farm equipment.

AFFILIATIONS

Member, Fresno County Automotive Repair & Mechanics Association
Member, Classic Chevrolet Car Owner's Association

Figure 4.6 Paralegal

SCOTT R. ALMADEN

3029 Pacheco Avenue
Sacramento, California 95608
(916) 560-3298 - scralm84@aol.com

FOCUS   *PARALEGAL – Articulate, poised legal professional with substantial education and experience in procedural law and research.*

SUMMARY OF QUALIFICATIONS

➢ *Areas of education and experience:* Legal Research and Writing, Discovery and Trial Preparation, Deposition Summation, Subpoena Preparation, Litigation, Law Office Practices, Torts and Contracts, Criminal Law, Business Law, and Business Organizations.

➢ *Computer skills:* Experienced in performing legal research utilizing California governmental databases and LexisNexis. Windows computer environment with MS Office Suite and WordPerfect-Legal Mode.

➢ *Degree:* Associate of Arts Degree and Certificate of Achievement in Paralegal Studies, Fresno City College.

➢ *Strengths:* Highly motivated and focused with excellent communication and organization skills.

➢ *Bilingual:* Read, write, and speak fluent Spanish.

PROFESSIONAL EXPERIENCE

Field Representative
WEST COAST LEGAL SERVICE, San Jose, California   **2011–Present**
• Maintain Fresno satellite office for service providing legal documents to residents in Central California.

Library Clerk
MCCORMICK, BARSTOW, SHEPPARD, & CARRUTH, Fresno, California   **2010–2011**
• Maintained law library, insuring that most recent cases and other legal resources were included in firm's legal collection.
• Performed limited legal research and assisted staff with word processing.

Office Assistant – Office of Admissions and Records
FRESNO CITY COLLEGE, Fresno, California   **2008–2010**
• Extensive interaction with students regarding admission, financial aid, and transcripts.

Field Representative
DOCUMENT COPY SERVICE, San Francisco, California   **2007**
• Served legal documents for clients and maintained Fresno office for company.

EDUCATION

Fresno City College, Fresno, California
Paralegal Certificate of Achievement and Associate of Arts Degree in Liberal Studies, 2011

Accomplishments: Academic scholarship recipient, fall, 2011; Dean's List, 2010 and 2011

Figure 4.7 Bookkeeper/Accounting Clerk

GUDDI P. DHILLON
9118 Lumont St., #104
Vancouver, WA 81729
(415) 612-4187
GPD122@aol.com

OBJECTIVE

CAREER POSITION AS BOOKKEEPER/ACCOUNTING CLERK

QUALIFICATIONS

- Associate of Science Degree in Accounting.

- Accounting program included courses in *Computer Accounting, Tax and Auditing, and Cost Accounting*.

- Performed all bookkeeping functions for 85-unit apartment complex while attending college full-time.

- Experienced in converting manual bookkeeping system to computer applications without downtime or significant problems.

- Knowledgeable regarding:
  Accounts Payable/Receivable
  General Ledger Entries
  Financial Statements
  Quarterly and Annual Payroll Tax Reporting
  Credit Applications and Verification Process

EDUCATION

Associate in Science Degree in Accounting   **May, 2012**
Clark College, Vancouver, WA

- GPA: 3.7 on a 4.0 scale
- Dean's List, 3 semesters
- Member, Accounting & Finance Fraternity

SKILLS

- Familiar with accounting and spreadsheet software (QuickBooks, Excel, Peachtree).

- Operate 10-key by touch.

- Well organized—complete projects accurately and in timely manner.

- Good listener and able to follow directions with minimum follow-up.

EMPLOYMENT

Bookkeeper/Assistant Manager   **2011–Present**
Sea Cliff Apartments,
Vancouver, WA
- Prepare payroll, bank deposits, financial statements, tax reports, and period-end reports.

Figure 4.8 Communications/Customer Service, Four-Year Degree

Marianne P. Moss

2343 Printer Way, Trenton, New Jersey 08608
(609) 196-5672 (C) ~ (609) 841-9937
Moss84@google.com

Career Focus

SALES AND TERRITORY MANAGEMENT – High-energy recent university graduate desires opportunity with respected organization that can benefit from a motivated, capable young professional with five years of experience in client-centered sales and service positions.

Profile

SALES	Progressively responsible sales/customer service experience assisting customers and utilizing suggestive sales techniques to increase revenue. Motivated by opportunity to serve clients and fulfill their needs.
CUSTOMER FOCUS	Able to easily establish client relationships built on exceptional service and thorough understanding of product knowledge.
GOAL ORIENTED	Set goals, devise plan, and follow through to achieve desired results. Creative problem solver with ability to learn client's unique needs and recommend solutions.
TECHNOLOGY	Computer proficient: MS Word/Excel, Internet Research, and QuickBooks.

Professional Experience

Customer Service / Admin. Assistant
Wells Fargo Securities, Trenton, NJ   3/2011–Present

➢ Part-time internship assisting senior VP with securities transactions. Manage follow-up regarding client concerns and questions, completion of appropriate financial forms, and account data entry.

Sales Associate – Part-time
Rachel's Boutique, Trenton, NJ   3/2010–Present

➢ Coordinate store operations and sales for small upscale clothing and home goods retail outlet.
➢ Attain sales goals and cultivate repeat business by providing outstanding service.
➢ Recommended adding trendy clothing lines that subsequently increased sales.

Personal Assistant / Nanny
Trenton, NJ   2008–Present

➢ Assist families with childcare; this entails planning/supervising age-appropriate programs, scheduling/transporting children to activities and appointments, and handling financial payments for children's expenses.

Customer Service Representative – Part-time
Starbucks, Trenton, NJ   2007–2008

➢ Selected to enter supervisor training program after only four months; declined promotion because of commitments to education and other part-time responsibilities.

Customer Service Representative / Front Desk
Harbor Inn, Atlantic City, NJ   2006–2007

➢ Performed front desk and concierge responsibilities for exclusive clientele at five-star resort.

Education

Bachelor of Arts Degree in Communications   2012
Thomas Edison State College, Trenton, NJ

Highlights:

➢ Financed partial living and education expenses while simultaneously working at more than one part-time position, completing university degree, and maintaining 3.2 GPA.

EXERCISE 4.1

Your Initial Draft

On the following two pages, please complete the simplified résumé format by filling in the appropriate information using Exercises 2.1 and 3.1 from Chapters 2 and 3. It is suggested that you initially write out a draft of your résumé on this page and the next. However, if you have a computer available, prepare the initial draft on your word processor. It will save you the time of having to transfer the information later.

(HEADING)
(YOUR NAME)_____
(Address)_____
(City, State) _____
(Phone) _____
(E-mail)_____

OBJECTIVE/FOCUS

_____
_____
_____

QUALIFICATIONS

_____
_____
_____
_____
_____
_____
_____
_____
_____

EDUCATION

_____
_____
_____
_____
_____
_____
_____

SKILLS

_____
_____

_____

_____

_____

LICENSES & CERTIFICATIONS

_____

_____

_____

EMPLOYMENT

_____

_____

_____

_____

_____

_____

_____

_____

_____

ORGANIZATIONS & ACTIVITIES

_____

_____

YOUR NAME

Your Address

OBJECTIVE

QUALIFICATIONS

EDUCATION

SKILLS

EMPLOYMENT

YOUR NAME

Your Address

OBJECTIVE

QUALIFICATIONS

EMPLOYMENT

EDUCATION

ORGANIZATIONS & ACTIVITIES

YOUR NAME

Your Address   **Your Phone and E-mail**

FOCUS

QUALIFICATIONS

EDUCATION

SKILLS

EMPLOYMENT

PROFESSIONAL LICENSES/CERTIFICATIONS/AFFILIATIONS

CHAPTER 5

Résumé Formats, Styles, and Applications

Learning Objectives

1. What is a scannable résumé, and how does it differ from a traditional résumé?
2. What type of employers request résumés that are scannable?
3. How do you convert your résumé prepared in MS Word to an Adobe PDF format, and what would be the benefit of converting it?
4. Of what value are job boards such as Monster.com and Careerbuilder.com? Are these the best sources of locating job opportunities?

INTRODUCTION

As you are probably aware, résumé formats, like most things in life, are changing with advances in technology. Today an employer may, upon receipt of your résumé, use a computer-related machine to scan and store your résumé for possible consideration at a later time.

It is also common for a prospective employer to ask you to either e-mail or fax a copy of your résumé. You can e-mail a résumé in a number of formats. One of the most common is attaching a word-processed document (usually Microsoft Word or Corel WordPerfect). You simply send (attach) a copy of the file that contains your résumé to an e-mail to a prospective employer. You can also convert your word-processed résumé to a different type of file (ASCII, RTF, or PDF) and then attach or include it within an e-mail.

As your career progresses, you may need to change the format of your résumé slightly. After you have two to five years of experience, it is advisable to emphasize the experience section of your résumé to a greater extent. The type of résumé format that places more emphasis on your work history is called a *chronological* résumé, which arranges positions by the dates of employment. Should you wish to change career fields after 10 years, you may need to develop what is termed a *functional* résumé, a résumé that emphasizes skills, not work history. Both of these types of résumés are discussed and/or illustrated on the following pages.

SCANNABLE RÉSUMÉS

Employers who recruit large numbers of new employees each year often use a scanner (computer-related hardware and software) that reads your résumé and stores its contents in a database to be quickly accessed if needed. Thus, the term "scannable résumé" has originated in the last few years—meaning a résumé that is prepared in a format ready to be scanned into a computer data base.

If you are submitting your résumé to large corporations such as Google, Ford Motor Co., Sears Roebuck, PG&E, Coca-Cola, Best Buy, Kaiser Permanente, or Intel Corporation, it will probably be scanned. In Chapter 8 there is an example of an online application for employment at Google. Note that it contains space where you can either paste or upload a résumé and another area where you can copy and paste a cover letter. All your application documents will be processed by a machine that will place them, along with hundreds or thousands of others, in a database. When a department within the company needs a particular position filled, the database is searched for a résumé(s) containing the skills or characteristics required for the position to be filled. The search is conducted by the computer hunting for *key words* in the résumés. If the position to be filled is that of a machinist, in addition to the word "machinist," key words would include: *tool and die, set up and operate conventional and special-purpose machines, fabricate metallic and nonmetallic parts, blueprints, specifications, determine tolerances of finished work piece, cutting tools, mills, lathes, jig borers, grinders, shapers, micrometers, height gauges, and gauge blocks, the number of years of experience, training on a certain manufacturer's equipment (Cincinnati Vertical with autofeed), schools attended, and where the applicant lives* may all be part of the key word search of the résumés on file. If your résumé has the required skills and characteristics for the job, it will be identified as one to be further reviewed to determine whether your qualifications are a good match for the position to be filled. It will then be printed and sent to the department in need of a machinist. If the qualifications on your résumé look good to the supervisor of the department, you may receive a call to come in for an interview. When this occurs, you should bring a presentation copy (professional-appearing copy as discussed and illustrated in the previous chapter) of your résumé with you, updated if appropriate.

Here are some additional tips on preparing a scannable résumé: Your résumé should always contain a qualifications section. However, in a résumé that will be scanned, it is best to focus on placing terms in the qualifications, skills, and employment sections that are commonly used and referred to in your occupation, like the ones listed in the machinist example above. Some résumé writers even suggest using a "key words" section, although we do not. The main focus in preparing a résumé—for scanning or otherwise—is to do your homework about the skills needed for the position. Find out the kinds of products, software, equipment, skills, and procedures that are commonly used in your occupation. Then be sure that you include these in the qualifications, skills, or employment section of your résumé. The scanning computer will pick them out regardless of where they appear in the résumé.

If you believe your résumé is to be scanned, it is best to:

1. Use white or a very light-colored paper if a hard copy is submitted.
2. Use a "True Type" font such as Arial or Times New Roman, point size 11 to 14.
3. Place your name on a single line on each page of the résumé.
4. Keep positions held, employer, and date of employment on separate lines.
5. Avoid using graphic lines, boxes, graphics, underlining, italics, and special symbols (solid bullets are okay).
6. Use an "align left" line setting (which produces an uneven right edge); avoid "justified" or "align right" settings as these settings squeeze letters.
7. Send either an unfolded copy of your résumé or a computer-faxed copy to the employer.

FAXING RÉSUMÉS

You may need to fax your résumé to a prospective employer. The employer may telephone and ask you to "fax your résumé" immediately. If this is the case, and you do not have a fax machine available, simply go to the local print/mailbox shop (such as FedEx/Kinko's). Most have fax machines for hire; the cost is usually about one dollar per page. Again, a résumé that is on white paper will fax with a cleaner look. After you have sent the fax, send a copy of your professional-appearing résumé on quality paper via the U.S. Postal Service—assuming you have the prospective employer's mailing address.

RÉSUMÉS SENT AS ATTACHMENTS

You may need to attach your résumé to an e-mail message. To attach a Word or WordPerfect file containing your résumé to an e-mail message, first open your e-mail program. After typing a brief message to the prospective employer stating the position for which you are applying and indicating that you are attaching your résumé to the e-mail, simply use the attachment feature of the e-mail program to add the file containing your résumé.

You will need to format your résumé so that it can be transmitted easily via e-mail and will appear at its destination in the same layout and design as you sent it. To do this, minimize formatting enhancements such as graphics, lines, and unique fonts to avoid problems on the receiving end.

Another way of sending your résumé via an attachment is to provide a digital copy of your résumé using PDF formatting. This is our preferred method of sending a résumé to a prospective employer. Adobe Acrobat, a software program available at most schools, is unique in that it literally takes a picture of your résumé that enables you to send an *exact* copy of your résumé—including any graphics, lines, symbols, and so on. It is the most accurate way to have an employer receive exactly what you sent. Adobe also has a free program called Adobe Reader that can be downloaded in few minutes. This program enables anyone to open and read a file that is in PDF format. Nearly everyone who owns a computer has the Adobe Reader software.

Whenever you intend to submit your résumé as an attachment to an e-mail, regardless of format, always send a trial e-mail to yourself with the attachment first to ensure that it comes through as intended.

POSTING RÉSUMÉS ON JOB BOARDS OR COMPANY SITES

You may be seeing some web addresses with the suffix ".jobs"; this is a new suffix that employers can use for job-posting web addresses. (The suffix has been approved by Icann, the nonprofit group that oversees Internet addresses.) This should make it easier for job seekers to go directly to a company link that has job postings. For example, rather than go to Union Pacific Railroad's main web address, http://www.up.com/, and then try to locate the job postings within the main site, you can use http://www.union-pacific.jobs/. In the future, we think many more companies will use the web address suffix.

If you are considering posting your résumé online to gain greater national exposure, this is how you do it. We will use Monster.com, the largest online job board, as an example. You must first establish an account with Monster.com as a "job seeker." You will need to choose a user name and password. You can then review job postings and place your personal résumé on the Monster site.

You can post your résumé on the Monster site in three ways. If you choose to "Build a Résumé," you write your résumé online by listing information about yourself in the sections provided. A second method is "Copy and Paste Text." This permits you to copy and paste material from an existing résumé (preferably in an ASCII or plain text format—to be explained later in this chapter) verbatim into the appropriate sections. The third method is to "Attach an Existing Résumé"; this enables you to place an entire Microsoft Word file containing your résumé online with Monster. The limitations with this method are that your résumé layout/formatting will not be retained, and you will not be able to edit the résumé online.

Most other corporate or institutional sites use one or more of these three methods. As will be further discussed in Chapter 10, *we believe it is more productive to post to company sites and diligently develop your networking skills.* These methods tend to be more productive than posting to national and international job boards.

CONVERTING YOUR RÉSUMÉ TO ASCII FORMAT

Sometimes you may wish to include your résumé as *part of* an e-mail message (not as an attachment) that you are sending to a prospective employer. Some employers prefer that your résumé be included in an e-mail as they are reluctant to open attachments because they may contain viruses. You might also want to post your résumé to some of the job banks or corporate databases discussed earlier. To do this, we suggest that you convert your résumé to what is known as "ASCII," or plain text format. An ASCII-formatted résumé looks like the one shown in Figure 5.1 of this chapter.

Converting to ASCII or plain text formatting will remove most of the *formatting enhancements, such as bold, italics, underlining, bullets, tab stops*, and so on. When you remove all the bullets, tab stops, and so on, the résumé often becomes longer and may require two pages. Do not be concerned about the length; when sending a résumé via e-mail, length is of little significance.

To convert a résumé, begin by opening your original résumé in your word processing program. Now click "Save As" in your word processor and select "Plain Text (*.txt)" in Word; in WordPerfect, select "ASCII DOS Text" as the file type in which to save the new format. Next, save this revised (very plain) résumé in a separate file and format using your word processing program. We also suggest you rename the file using a name that reflects this "very plain" plain text/ASCII résumé. After saving the document in this format, close the document and then reopen it to see whether all the changes you have made remain. Then tweak it: make some changes by placing the name of the job you are seeking at the very top of the résumé above your name, adding double spaces between sections of the résumé, and using only keys on the keyboard (*, +, >, -, ~) to enhance or highlight parts of the résumé (see the example below). Capitals can be used effectively. Shorten the line to 60 spaces or five inches. Finally, hit the Enter or Return key after each line so that you have hard returns after each line. After making these changes and again saving your document, select or block the copy and paste it into an e-mail. Try sending an e-mail to yourself to see if the résumé needs any further tweaking. Remember, this type of résumé is to be included within the e-mail, not attached to the e-mail. Last, you will need to save the "Plain Text" résumé again. Reopen the résumé and note that all the changes have remained except the line spacing, which has reverted to the initial settings. Note the example on the next page (Figure 5.1). This is the same résumé that appeared on page 35 of Chapter 4.

CHRONOLOGICAL/FUNCTIONAL STYLE RÉSUMÉS

Résumé formats are usually described as either *chronological* or *functional*. A chronological résumé emphasizes your employment history. It is organized in reverse chronological (time) order—the last job appearing first. Thus, the name "chronological" means that your former positions appear in reverse chronology, according to dates of employment.

This type of format is used if you have substantial employment background and have remained in the same occupation. For example, assume you began work right out of school as a payroll clerk and have been in that occupation for 15 years. Now assume that the company you worked for has been sold, and you need either to reapply or seek work elsewhere. In this instance, it would be best to use a chronological résumé format because long-term employment in the same occupation is considered a strength.

Figure 5.1 ASCII/E-mail Résumé

MARKETING ASSISTANT POSITION

RAMONA E. BROOKS
1218 E. Montecito, Apt. 19
Fresno, CA 93707
(559) 225-0404
reb500@hotmail.com

QUALIFICATIONS

* Associate Degree in Business Administration, Marketing emphasis.
* Three years of customer service experience in retail settings.
* Experience planning and implementing special promotions, including flyers, advertising copy, and special displays for major retailer's cosmetic department.
* Computer/software skills: Dreamweaver, Corel Presentations, and MS FrontPage, Word, Excel, and PowerPoint software; keyboarding speed: 50+ WPM.
* Excellent problem-solving ability; work well under pressure; creative in use of graphics and drawing—freehand and with custom software.
* Team player; interact well with coworkers and management—completed courses in human relations, communications, and supervision.

EMPLOYMENT

Cosmetics Counter Manager
2011 to Present
J. C. PENNEY, Fresno, CA

> Earned "All Star" award for consistently meeting or exceeding monthly and yearly quotas.

> Plan and implement special promotions, including flyers, advertising copy, and special displays.

> Process orders, product returns, and resolve customer service concerns.

Payroll Assistant
2009–2011
Twelfth Street Courier Service, Everett, MS

> Utilized computer accounting system to prepare payroll, accounts payable/receivable, and bank reconciliation.

EDUCATION

Associate of Arts Degree in Business Administration, 2012
Fresno City College, Fresno, CA

Maintained 3.2 GPA while working full-time.
Earned 100% of living and education expenses.

Activities:
  Alpha Gamma Sigma (Fresno City College Honor Society)

  Treasurer, Students in Free Enterprise (SIFE)

  Volunteer, Ronald McDonald House

In essence, *after stating your objective and qualifications* in the résumé, it would be appropriate to list your employment in reverse chronological order.

What about the *functional* format? This type of format is used when you do not have a long work history in the area where you are seeking employment or you are moving into a new occupational area. Using the preceding example, if after 15 years as a payroll clerk you decided to seek employment as a forest ranger, you will need to have something more than 15 years of payroll experience. Hopefully, you have been attending school at night to study forestry management and/or zoology, and have joined the Sierra Club. And maybe you have been a scout master or hiker who has explored significant mountain ranges and other National Forest preserves during vacations or while on leave from your employer. In this situation, you would place your education and the activities that relate to employment with the forest service *after the objective and qualifications section* of your résumé.

Both types of résumé formats focus on putting your most relevant qualifications near the top of the résumé, remembering to list *only* the skills, education, knowledge, and qualifications that are important in qualifying you for that particular job.

CHAPTER 6

Researching Prospective Employers Online and Tips on Salary Negotiations

Learning Objectives

1. What percentage of America's largest employers post job openings online?
2. How can doing research regarding a company that you are considering for possible employment be helpful if and when you are interviewed by that company?
3. Where can you research general salary information or wage information for a specific company? How and where can this information be used?

RESEARCHING ONLINE EMPLOYMENT OPPORTUNITIES

Employers are more likely to post their primary job openings on their own web page or on sites that focus on occupations within their industry as opposed to placing an advertisement in the classifieds. They believe their own site or industry sites will bring in candidates with better qualifications. Thus, interested job applicants should focus their online search on specific employer sites, industry associations, or trade publications. An article in *SmartMoney*, a *Wall Street Journal* publication, indicated that 434 of the 500 largest companies in the United States post jobs on their own websites. More recent sources indicate that perhaps as many as 99 percent of Fortune 500 companies post employment opportunities on their own website.

TARGETED APPROACH

We suggest that you use a targeted approach to research job opportunities online. A targeted approach focuses on specific companies that you would like to work for, or, at a minimum, specific industries that you wish to focus on. An impressive site that will help you identify targeted web locations is the Riley Guide (http://www.rileyguide.com/), which has an abundance of resources related to targeting specific companies and employer groupings (for example, the *Fortune* 500 listing is: http://money.cnn.com/magazines/fortune/fortune500/2010/index.html). For information, refer to the job listings subsection on the site. One of the individuals responsible for the Riley Guide, Margaret Riley Dikel, has written *Guide to Internet Job Searching 2008–2009,* a paperback that provides an excellent guide to researching companies on the web.

An excellent site that focuses on how to research private companies was developed by the Library of Congress (http://www.loc.gov/rr/business/company/private.html). This site takes you step-by-step through the process of researching private and public employers and has a multitude of additional resources and lists for conducting online research. A comprehensive site for allied health occupations (http://allied.health.jobs.topusajobs.com/) has listings for employment opportunities throughout the

United States. The same site also lists employment opportunities by location in other industries as well.

If you explore the websites of major employers in your community, you will frequently find postings for positions that interest you. Civil service opportunities (positions in governmental agencies within city, county, state, and federal bureaus) are nearly always posted and provide an excellent starting point for new graduates. Government agencies often equate educational achievement with experience and thus make landing an entry-level position without experience much more likely than in the private sector. Employment in private enterprise often becomes more accessible after a couple of years in government service.

The JobCentral National Employment Network (http://www.jobcentral.com/) is an alliance between two nonprofit associations, the DirectEmployers Association and the National Association of Colleges and Employers (NACE), to provide job seekers in all industries and occupations—from entry-level to chief executive officer—with up-to-date information about employment and career opportunities nationwide. You can place a résumé and cover letter on this site without a fee. You can use the site without registering, and when you find a listing that interests you, you are directed to the employer's website to review the listing and apply.

If you are interested in companies that have achieved status as being desirable to work for, you might consider visiting *Fortune* Magazine's 2010 "100 Best Companies to Work For," http://money.cnn.com/magazines/fortune/bestcompanies/2010/. Many local communities have publications that imitate *Fortune*'s 100 Best Companies. To find these, it is best to do a Google or Yahoo search, listing something like, "best companies to work for in (name of your city)."

EXAMPLES OF JOB LISTINGS ON THE INTERNET

This first job listing is from the county government unit in Harris County (Houston), Texas (http://www.hctx.net/hrrm/Technical.aspx).

ANNOUNCEMENT NUMBER: 14479-T

JOB TITLE: Medical Assistant*

DEPARTMENT: Public Health & Environmental Services
Refugee Health Program

HOURS: 8:00 a.m. – 5:00 p.m. / Monday – Friday

SALARY: Commensurate With Qualifications

EDUCATION: High school diploma or G.E.D. equivalent is required. Completion of a Medical Assistant or Certified Nurse's Aide program from a community college or business/technical school is required.

EXPERIENCE: Six months of experience as a Medical or Nurse Assistant in a medical office, hospital, or laboratory is required.

JOB SKILLS: Successful candidate must be proficient in adult and pediatric phlebotomy; possess good oral communication and data entry skills, have basic knowledge in operation of a personal computer. Ability to communicate fluently in any other foreign language(s) in addition to English is preferred.

JOB DESCRIPTION: Assists with patient screening by performing phlebotomy (including capillary, venous, and heel stick samples), urine collection and pregnancy tests, vital signs, heights and weights. Prepares and labels samples for transport to appropriate laboratories. Provides in-room support and assistance to the nurses/physicians during the clinic session as appropriate. Inventories supplies and submits items for order, as needed. Rotates dated stock to prevent loss of outdated supplies. Maintains laboratory and exam rooms in a clean and orderly manner. Assists in performing data entry, electronic data processing and data quality control activities related to the maintenance of the electronic TB/Refugee data collection and/or record system, including the entry of patient registration encounters and appointments. Assembles records/charts in preparation for Refugee Program health clinics. Faxes, files lab reports and other medical forms. Demonstrates cultural sensitivity in serving patients of varied ethnic and socioeconomic backgrounds. Performs other duties as assigned, including special tasks involved in responding to an emergency event.

Position requires the ability to lift twenty five pounds.

*GRANT FUNDED

EMPLOYMENT IS CONTINGENT UPON PASSING A CRIMINAL BACKGROUND CHECK.

HARRIS COUNTY HAS AN EMPLOYMENT AT WILL POLICY.

CLOSING DATE: Open Until Filled

APPLY AT: 1310 PRAIRIE, SUITE 170

UPON RECEIVING A CONDITIONAL OFFER OF EMPLOYMENT, ALL APPLICANTS ARE SCREENED FOR THE PRESENCE OF ILLEGAL DRUGS.
- Applications should be typed or printed (black or blue ink only).
- Résumés will not be accepted as a substitute for applications.
- Incomplete applications will not be accepted.
- All statements made on the application (s) are subject to investigation and/or verification.
- Applicants may apply for multiple positions by submitting separate applications for each position. Applicants may make as many copies as desired. Copies, however, cannot be provided by HRRM.

SUBMITTING YOUR APPLICATION BY MAIL
- Announcement number and job title MUST be recorded on the application.
- Applications by facsimile or e-mail are not accepted at this time.
- Applications for positions requiring testing (Clerical Skills Test) will not be accepted unless current scores are on file.

Two additional examples are from a major U.S. and global employer, Stanley Black and Decker Corporation (http://www.stanleyblackanddecker.com/) which is headquartered in New Britain, Connecticut. Stanley Black and Decker, an S&P 500 company, is a diversified global provider of hand tools, power tools and related accessories, small appliances, mechanical access solutions and electronic security solutions, engineered fastening systems, and more. It employs several thousand people, has a wide range of career positions, offers excellent benefits, and provides incentives for continued education. Stanley Black and Decker is considered a very progressive and well-respected employer in the United States. At the time of this writing, Stanley Black and Decker's home page had nearly 200 positions listed under career opportunities. Here are two examples:

Technical Illustrator

Position Summary

Job Title:	Technical Illustrator
Division:	Kwikset
Position Status:	Full Time
Position Type:	Regular
Country:	U.S.
State:	California
City:	Lake Forest

Region or Territory:

JOB DESCRIPTION: Stanley Black & Decker, an S&P 500 company, is a diversified global provider of hand tools, power tools and related accessories, mechanical access solutions and electronic security solutions, engineered fastening systems, and more.

We hire, develop, and reward great people who understand the importance of a strong culture that values integrity, commitment, teamwork, and diversity. Our employees have a passion for developing great products and innovative solutions that meet our customers' needs. By satisfying customers, we improve people's lives, and by doing so, create value for our stockholders—providing a great future for our customers, our company, and our employees.

The Stanley Black & Decker Hardware and Home Improvement Group (HHI) is part of the company's Security division. HHI develops, manufactures, markets and sells builders hardware, residential and commercial door hardware, kitchen and bath faucets, shower systems and bath accessories under the Stanley, National Hardware, Kwikset, Weiser, Baldwin, K2 and Price Pfister brands. Headquartered in Orange County, California, HHI has a global sales force and operates manufacturing and distribution facilities in the US, Canada, Mexico, and Asia. Our people enjoy a business casual work environment in which individual development is encouraged. As a billion dollar business within Stanley Black & Decker, we are able to provide both the growth opportunities of a large company and the visibility and exposure of a small organization.

SUMMARY: As the Technical Illustrator, you will work directly with the New Product Introduction teams of engineers and marketing product managers. Having minimal supervision, you will produce graphic material by performing a variety of support tasks in the planning, layout, and preparation of commercial art work for inclusion in product installation instructions, installation template, proposals, technical manuals, product brochures, displays, presentations, slides and similar graphics applications.

MAJOR DUTIES AND RESPONSIBILITIES (ESSENTIAL FUNCTIONS):

1. Executes assigned projects, producing sketches, drawings and other illustrative material according to instructions and specific parameters developed by others.
2. Selects techniques best suited to produce desired visual effects in conformance with specified quality standards.

Technical Illustrator *(continued)*

3. Determines composition, view angles, perspective, projections, etc.
4. Utilizes and applies a variety of graphic techniques including line illustrations, isometrics, perspectives, orthographic, block diagrams, renderings, graphs, schematics and the like.
5. Plans complete layouts for finished graphics.
6. Translates illustrative objectives into graphic terms.
7. Creates department procedures and work instructions.

EMPLOYEE SPECIFICATIONS (MINIMUM QUALIFICATIONS):

Education and Work Experience:

- Associate's degree from an accredited college or technical school with classes in technical illustration, art, drafting, or equivalent.
- Four years' experience working with graphic material, sketches, and drawings.

Technical/Functional Competencies:

- In-depth knowledge of products within SBDHHI business unit.
- Skilled with graphics production equipment and supplies, including personal computers and desktop publishing/graphics software such as Adobe Creative Suite and/or other vector-based software programs.
- Knowledge of Pro/Engineer or other Solid Modeling CAD software.
- Work independently using considerable creative judgment regarding composition, media selection and the like.
- Ability to work independently, as a team member and as a team leader.
- Solid understanding of printing and production processes.
- Outstanding communication and interpersonal skills.
- Ability to determine priorities and manage multiple projects at one time.
- Flexibility in schedule in order to meet hard deadlines.
- Consumer Products industry experience preferred.

Stanley Black & Decker offers its employees a competitive salary and a comprehensive benefits plan that includes medical, dental, life, disability, 401k, vacation, paid holidays, and more!

Apply now to join an organization that has been named as Orange County Register's Top Work Places 2008 & 2009 (Top 50), and OC Business Journal's Best Places to Work 2009 (Top 40).

Equal Opportunity Employer M/F/D/V
GREAT PEOPLE. GREAT PRODUCTS. GREAT FUTURE.

Technical Illustrator

Bilingual Field Coordinator

Job Title: Bilingual Field Coordinator

Division: Power Tools

Position Status: Full Time

Position Type: Regular

Country: U.S.

State: California

City: San Diego

Region or Territory:

JOB DESCRIPTION: Description

You know the jobsites, you know the contractors, you know the tools: turn that knowledge into a stable, long term career with a large, Fortune 500 Power Tool company.

Join DEWALT High Performance Industrial Power Tools. . .
DEWALT is firmly committed to being the best in the business, and this commitment to being number one extends to everything we do, from product design and engineering to manufacturing and service. A big part of how we make sure our tools are "the best" is spending time with our end users, listening to their needs and concerns and discovering new and better ways to get the job done.

In a highly focused role . . .
We are looking for a bilingual (English/Spanish) candidate with construction and sales experience. In this position, you will work with our end users (or contractors) in the field to increase DEWALT brand and product awareness and, over time, market share. Your focus will be interacting with end users in the places they "Buy, Work, Learn and Play" such as retail outlets, construction jobsites, trade associations, lifestyle events, promotions, and DEWALT sponsored events. You will share product knowledge, demonstrate and seed products, provide samples, create excitement around the brand and more.

With great rewards . . .
By joining DEWALT, you will enjoy:
A high profile role within a Fortune 500 corporation praised as one of Fortune Magazine's Most Admired Brands.
Job stability and regular hours.
A full benefits package including medical, dental, vision, and 401(k) from the day you start.
A company vehicle.
Opportunity for career advancement.
The flexibility of working from a home office with all administrative expenses included.
Salary Range $40,000 - $48,000 a year, commensurate with experience.

Technical Illustrator (*continued*)

Our Requirements
Bilingual (English and Spanish)
College Degree Preferred.
Solid construction industry experience (at least 2 years).
Construction contacts in the local community.
A high level of motivation.
US Resident or Citizen.

More About the Position
You will be a part of a field marketing team that is focused on expanding DEWALT brand and product awareness and use within the construction community. Reporting to a Field Marketing Manager, you will base yourself from a home office and cover a territory that includes San Diego.

You will start with a comprehensive training program at corporate headquarters followed up with specific training with your field marketing team. You will be well prepared before you head out into the field, and your manager will be actively involved in your ongoing learning and development.

Once training is complete you will spend about 80% of your time on jobsites, retail events and lifestyle events, and the balance on administrative tasks in your home office. Of the time you spend in the field, the majority will be visiting construction jobsites and interacting with contractors.

Your overall goals include:
Increasing DEWALT's market share on jobsites within your territory.
Creating greater brand and product awareness in the market through product demonstrations at sports and other events.
Driving and supporting Promotions at distribution.
Promoting and driving new users to our Product Service Network.
Providing critical end-user feedback to our product team.

Your responsibilities will include:
Providing hands on demos and loaner tools to drive conversions on construction jobsites.
Delivering Tool Safety Training to users and companies.
Supporting key initiatives and promotions with our distribution partners, such as: working both inside the store as well as with outside distributor sales reps and at jobsite events;
participating in DEWALT sponsored events that promote the brand such as boxing and soccer events; and
participating in events with contractor associations, vocational schools, Power Tool safety events, etc.
Driving new products and promotions with key users and jobsites.
Driving Product Service Center awareness and new customers.
Product Manager "work with" which involve spending time gathering feedback on tools and new product features with end users.

Technical Illustrator

As you can see, this role will put you on the front lines of our sales and marketing team, and you'll be responsible for millions of dollars in business. In addition to impacting thousands of customers, you'll see first hand what works and what doesn't in our marketing and product strategies. The feedback you'll provide will help shape those strategies, and over time, enable you to build a name for yourself within our organization.

If this sounds like the right mix of challenge and opportunity for you, and you meet the requirements, we look forward to hearing from you!

Who We Are
About DEWALT
DEWALT is a leading manufacturer of industrial power tools with more than 300 power tool and equipment products as well as 800 power tool accessories, including corded and cordless drills, saws, hammers, grinders, routers, planers, plate joiners, sanders, lasers, generators, compressors and nailers, as well as saw blades, metal and masonry drill bits, abrasives, screw driving accessories and more. DEWALT tools can be found wherever tools are sold, nationally and internationally. With over 1,000 factory owned and authorized locations, DEWALT has one of the most extensive service and repair networks in North America.

About Stanley Black & Decker
Stanley Black & Decker is a global marketer and manufacturer of quality products used in and around the home and for commercial applications. We hire, develop, and reward great people who understand the importance of a strong culture that values integrity, commitment, teamwork, and diversity. We are a Fortune 500 company and are ranked as one of Fortune Magazine's Most Admired Companies.

Our employees have a passion for developing great products and innovative solutions that meet our customers' needs. By satisfying customers, we improve people's lives, and by doing so, create value for our stockholders — providing a great future for our customers, our company, and our employees.

The Power Tools and Accessories segment manufactures and markets power tools, lawn and garden products, portable power products, home products, and accessories under the Stanley Black & Decker®, DEWALT®, Porter-Cable® and Delta® names, as well as other trademarks and trade names. This segment also provides product service and operates factory outlet stores. Headquartered in Towson, Maryland, this segment accounted for sales in 2008 of more than $4.3 billion.

We are an equal opportunity employer. EOE M/F/D/V

Note that information is given regarding the skills required for each position, the location of employment, minimum education, and the medium to use to complete the employment process. Almost all of the initial employment contacts are online.

If you were interested in any of the positions with either Harris County or Stanley Black and Decker, it would be appropriate to do more research on their respective websites before completing an application and submitting a résumé. An applicant can generally get a sense from the website of how large the agency/company is, what its mission statement is, where its offices are located, what the main services or products are, perhaps what the pay range and benefits are for some positions, the types of positions currently available, and other significant information.

BENEFITS OF ONLINE RESEARCH

You can use company or government agency information to influence hiring decisions in several ways. First, a mention in an e-mail or cover letter that you have some knowledge of the agency or company—that you have completed some research—and have some specific knowledge about what they do and how you might fit in with their mission will be very well received. Second, you can use some of your new-found information during the interview process. You will want to make reference to information (mission statement, number of employees, type of training available to employees, and so on) that you found on their web page in your responses to questions during the interview. A young friend of ours was about to be interviewed for a position as a merchandiser with Nabisco, the cookie/cracker company. Just prior to the interview, he stopped at a supermarket and went to the section displaying Nabisco products. He noted two or three products produced by Nabisco that he had not seen before. He asked a nearby clerk about these items and was told that they were new products that had only been on the shelf a week. He jotted down the names of these new products on a piece of paper and memorized them. During the subsequent interview, he mentioned these items to the interviewer. The interviewer was so impressed that he had done this research and learned of these products that a job offer was made on the spot. It pays to do your homework.

Using the Internet in your job search demonstrates to an employer that you possess leading-edge computer research skills. Whether you found the job listing online or did research online before your interview, make sure you communicate this to the prospective employer. It tells them you not only know how to use a computer, but you also know how to navigate the challenges of doing online research.

Another positive thing about conducting a job search online is that it makes it relatively easy to find employment in locations other than where you live. You can find job postings in almost every city and county in the United States by going on the Internet and looking at online classifieds for a particular city or region. You simply need to find out the name of the local newspaper in that location and then look at the help wanted ads. To be interviewed you may have to take a day off from work to travel to the city where you are seeking employment, but in some instances this may be accomplished online as well.

Another technique for finding a position either locally or in another city is to place a classified advertisement stating the position you want and your primary qualifications. You can accomplish this online by using free services such as Craigslist in your city (for example, at http://chicago.craigslist.org/ in the Chicago area), or a new free service sponsored by Wal-Mart (http://www.oodle.com/job/), which is also regional by city and state. And another new site that enables you to search by location and for specific positions is Indeed.com. You can also look at the "jobs" section in any of these free online services.

The technology today (company and government home pages, Google, Yahoo!, Monster, and so on) provides a wealth of information, and it is at your fingertips. We suggest you use it!

SALARY INFORMATION ONLINE

It is wise to have a good idea of the prevailing wage being paid for a particular type of work in the city where you want to be employed. There are several ways to gather this information. Certainly some of the most accessible sources will be found online. JobCentral (http://jobcentral.salary.com/) has an easy-to-use salary wizard. The Riley Guide mentioned earlier has substantial salary information, as do Monster.com and Careerbuilder.com.

When doing research regarding wages, you must be careful to distinguish between entry-level salaries and those of long-term employees. The distinction can be substantial, such as what an apprentice earns when learning the plumbing trade and the rate paid to a journeyman plumber. The variance can be as much as 100 percent or more.

SALARY NEGOTIATIONS

Here are a couple of suggestions about negotiating for compensation and benefits during the interview phase. First, do your homework. Have solid information regarding the typical wage that the company where you are applying pays someone with your qualifications. If you cannot find the information online or through local government labor/employment agencies, then try to connect with someone who works for the company. Use your network of friends and relatives and ask if they know anyone who works there. If you learn of someone, ask him to introduce you so that you can ask a few questions? One of the questions would be, "What is the typical starting salary for this position?"

Don't initiate salary discussions during the interview! When you are seriously being considered for employment with a firm, you will be offered a salary normally paid to someone with your background. Through your research, you should be able to determine what this figure will be. However, at this point, you can negotiate the salary if you think you merit a higher wage than offered. However, never commence negotiating a salary figure until you have been offered the job. Once you learn that the company is interested in you, you then have some leverage to negotiate. If you do decide to make a counteroffer, indicate what your special qualifications are that justify earning more than their initial offer. If your proposal is reasonable and justified, you will usually get some or all of what you requested. However, do not justify your request for more money by saying that you *need* or *feel* you should receive a greater wage. Your justification has to be on the basis of your qualifications and how your abilities will generate more revenue for the company. Most companies have a range for all jobs, even beginning jobs. Thus, they may offer you $14 per hour or $2600 per month to begin. However, they may be authorized to pay up to $16 per hour or $2800 per month, and will do so if the candidate is special and merits additional compensation. The $14 figure is for the average new employee, not the exceptional one. Are you the exceptional one?

An example of salary negotiations for a recent graduate is as follows. The new graduate was an accounting major, had completed an internship with a regional accounting firm, possessed a 3.86 GPA in accounting, and had already taken the CPA exam (results were pending). After three interviews with one of the nation's largest accounting firms, the new accounting graduate received an offer of employment as a field auditor. The offer was in the low 50s (thousand). It seemed quite adequate, especially since she had been living a very modest lifestyle while completing her college education. When the graduate enthusiastically told her father about the offer, he suggested she make a counteroffer to the initial salary offer. She was shocked by his assertiveness in this situation. Her father was a building contractor and explained that most things are accomplished in the business community through negotiation—a give and take and some degree of compromise. Whether you should negotiate depends on your strengths, and on the cards you have to play in the negotiation game. This young woman had several cards to play: experience from her internship, a strong grade point average in her major, and her gender—the company was, as are many companies, interested in boosting the number of female employees on its accounting staff, a typically male-dominated profession. With the support of her father, she mustered the courage to counteroffer, asking for an additional $4,000 per year. Her counter proposal was granted without question or further discussion. Do remember, you need to have strong cards to play to become a winner in the negotiation game.

What are your salary expectations after one or two years with the company? This is another point you might wish to negotiate with HR (human resources) and/or your immediate supervisor during the initial employment phase. If you would like to earn $19 per hour at the end of two years, we suggest you begin negotiating that at the start of your employment. The way to begin this conversation is start with a question such as, "What type of training and job responsibilities do I need at the end of two years to be earning $19 per hour?" Listen carefully, restate what you have been told, and be sure to validate the response with your immediate supervisor if this discussion took place with HR. You will have established the basis for your first raise. It will also eliminate the guess work normally associated with salaries and promotions in a new position. You will now have a more realistic view of salary expectations for the next few years.

EXERCISE 6.1

Online Employment Opportunities

Go online and find the website for your city or county government. Now find the employment opportunities section and copy a minimum of two positions that you believe you are currently qualified for or will be qualified for when you complete your current college training program. Then describe any skills described in the positions that you need to acquire before being fully qualified for either of the positions. Where can you obtain training in the skills that you will need for this position?

Cover Letters

Learning Objectives

1. What type of material is included in the cover letter that may not appear in the résumé or application?
2. How should you use information found in your research about a company in the cover letter?
3. What should your letterhead contain, and how long should a cover letter be?
4. What is a job announcement? What does it contain? Where are job announcements found?

Why do we write cover letters to accompany our résumés, and why are they called cover letters? The purpose of the cover letter is to personalize the application process and state the *specific* skills you have that are required for the position you are seeking. It spotlights your unique qualifications for a particular job. Since it covers (is placed on top of) the résumé, it is called a cover letter. It is often the first part of your presentation that a prospective employer will see. When you meet others for the first time, your eyes usually focus on their face. The face of your application materials is the cover letter, so put on your best face and write a dynamic cover letter to make a great first impression.

The cover letter should:

1. Be directed to a specific individual if possible.
2. Be well researched and well written—focused on the specific requirements of the position for which you are applying (duties listed in the job description obtained online or elsewhere).
3. State only your very best qualifications.
4. Request a meeting/interview with the potential employer.

WRITE TO A SPECIFIC INDIVIDUAL

Try to direct your cover letter to a specific person. If possible, you want to get your letter/résumé into the hands of the person who is doing the hiring. If you are asked to reply to the Human Resources Department (HRD) and you can also determine the name of the manager who will be making the final hiring decision, send a letter and résumé to each. Be sure the company and individual names/titles are spelled correctly.

COMPANY AND JOB KNOWLEDGE

It is best to know something about the organization to which you are applying. If it is a large company, your best bet is to conduct research regarding the firm by using the Internet, as described in Chapter 6. Also, the research librarian in most libraries will be glad to help you find information about the company. If it is a small local enterprise, you may visit the local newspaper office to find articles published about the company in the last two or three years. If nothing has been published, call the Human Resources (HR) department or receptionist at the firm and ask if they have a descriptive brochure or annual report that provides background on the company's products or services. The company may be pleased that you inquired and will be glad to send you current information. The better informed you are about the business—what it does, where its plants/offices are located, number of employees, and growth pattern—the better prepared you will be to write a cover letter describing *how you fit into the company's future*. This same information about the organization will be very valuable in preparing for the interview (see Chapter 11).

In addition, you need to know the duties and responsibilities of the job for which you are applying. If you learn of a potential position through an online posting or the newspaper and just an e-mail address or post office box is listed for replies, you may have only the information contained in the advertisement. However, if the company name is listed and there are only limited details regarding the job responsibilities for this position, it may be best to contact their HR department. Ask HR whether they have a "job announcement" sheet that they can forward to you or if the position has been posted online. The job announcement sheet usually lists the required experience, skills, education, and knowledge needed for the advertised position.

The purpose in learning the *specific* job requirements is to enable you to respond to these skill requirements in your cover letter. If one of the requirements for a clerical position is knowledge of WordPerfect Office X5 to format newsletters, you would do well to include in your cover letter that you are experienced in using this particular program. If you have prepared a monthly newsletter for the past 18 months using this program, that should be included in the cover letter. In other words, when you discover the employer's job requirements, it is essential to *describe the qualifications you possess that match these requirements*. This is the essence of a good cover letter.

INCLUDE YOUR BEST QUALIFICATIONS

What should you include in the letter? Your best qualifications! These are the *skills, knowledge, experience, education, and attitudes that most closely relate to the job requirements* that were listed in the job announcement. Will some of these also appear in the résumé? Yes. Because the letter is often the first communication read, it is okay to again highlight the qualifications you possess that relate to the job's requirements. It is also best to state in the cover letter any unique qualifications you possess that other applicants may not have. If the clerical position mentioned earlier requiring WordPerfect Office X5 is for employment with a parochial school and you have volunteered in your church's office for the past two summers, it would be best to state that you have clerical experience in a church office. Normally, one does not include religious affiliations in a résumé, but if the position is in a religious setting, experience working in a church office might be appropriate to include—unless the religious affiliations are incompatible.

REQUEST AN INTERVIEW

When ending a cover letter, it is appropriate to request an interview. This should be a positive statement: "I welcome the opportunity to meet with you to further describe my qualifications for the clerical opening in the church's administrative offices." You might go on to say, "I can be reached at the above phone number after 2 p.m. daily, or a message may be left at the same number." Another way of ending a cover letter is to state, "I will call you within a few days to arrange a time for us to meet and answer any questions you might have regarding my qualifications; I am excited about the opportunity to work in an office where integrity and values will be foremost."

SAMPLE COVER LETTERS

On the following pages are five cover letters. The format used in cover letters is as follows:

1. *Letterhead*—the heading should begin on the fourth line from the top edge of the page (not margin) and should be identical to the heading appearing on your résumé. You can copy and paste it if you like. The only difference in the letter's heading is that it is only one-half inch from the top of the page while the résumé normally is one inch from the top of the page.
2. *Body*—the body of the letter is single spaced with an unjustified right margin (uneven right edge), and there is a double space between paragraphs. More information about formatting the letter appears in the instructions for Exercise 7.1 appearing at the end of this chapter.
3. *First paragraph*—identifies the position for which you are applying and is positive in tone.
4. *Second paragraph*—describes the candidate's qualifications that are needed in the position you are applying for—your strongest skills and experience. Your résumé should be referred to at the end of this paragraph. Sometimes an additional paragraph may be needed to elaborate on your qualifications or to indicate that you have some specific knowledge that might be useful to the company, such as a foreign language, specialized training, or travel.
5. *Third paragraph*—requests an interview or states your intention to call for an interview time in the next few days.

Each of the cover letters on the following pages has been successfully used to obtain interviews (although the names and addresses are fictional). The letters are all positive in tone and indicate qualifications that the letter writer has that will be of value to the company where employment is sought. After a review of the letters, prepare a draft of a cover letter for yourself (Exercise 7.1 at the end of the chapter). Make sure the letter states *what you can do for the employer, not what the employer can do for you.*

The first letter is written in response to an advertisement/job announcement obtained from the Sunday employment section of a major California newspaper. The announcement reads as follows:

ADMINISTRATIVE ASSISTANT Great opportunity for administrative assistant in professional, fast-paced CPA office with congenial staff. Candidate should possess multi-line phone experience, have pleasant voice and good English skills, be comfortable with MS Word and Excel, and type 45 WPM. Extended hours required during tax season. Applicant should have Associate Degree or Certification as an Administrative Assistant. Forward résumé to CPA Group, 8644 N. Woodrow Ave., Fresno, CA 93711.

The letter on the following page is written with the purpose of indicating that the applicant has all or nearly all of the skills required for the position. In addition, a positive tone shows that the writer is willing to work overtime during tax season and has the social skills to successfully relate to the other employees in the office.

Anita P. Ramirez

1216 Adoline Street   559-237-9860
Clovis, CA 93260   apr22@cvip.net

January 16, 2012

CPA Group
8644 N. Woodrow Avenue
Fresno, CA 93711

RE: Administrative Assistant Position

I was excited to read about the employment opportunity within your office. Many of the
skills required for this position are those that I believe I possess. I especially like the focus
on working with a congenial staff as that is so important and makes going to work each day
fun and interesting.

My degree in Office Occupations (Administrative Assistant Option) was obtained in December
of 2011 from Kings River Community College. Some of the skill sets I acquired while in the
program include:
- Keyboarding/typing – certificate received for 57 WPM with 1 error on 5 minute test
- Ability to format correspondence and other documents using MS Word
- Development, modification, and utilization of spreadsheets using MS Excel
- Applications and practice using a multi-line phone system

This letter is an example of my writing and English language abilities. Additional information
regarding my training and background is available on the attached résumé.

While attending college, I worked 25 hours each week in a dental office where I performed
a variety of tasks, including scheduling appointments, preparing insurance claims, greeting
patients, and assisting other office personnel with their assignments. I have been asked to
stay on in this position, but prefer a full-time rather than a part-time position. In addition,
I have no hesitancy about working overtime during the tax season.

Please call me at the above number and we can schedule a time for me to meet with you to
further discuss my qualifications and experience.

Sincerely,

Anita P. Ramirez

Enclosure

PATRICIA SINGH

714 Garrison Square
Oakland, CA 95361
(408) 792-1325
pos761@aol.com

July 17, 2012

Human Resources Department
Hershey's Chocolate
75 East Derry Road
Hershey, PA 17033

RE: ACCOUNTS PAYABLE POSITION, Hershey's Chocolate of California, Inc.

Please accept my résumé and consider me a candidate for the position of Accounts Payable Clerk. Your recent job posting must have been written with me in mind as the experience and skills I possess are very closely aligned with those for the position you described.

I am a detail-oriented, well-organized accounting assistant who gets along well with staff members and management. As you seek a well-prepared assistant for your accounting department, please consider my qualifications:

- One year part-time experience in payroll, invoicing, and general bookkeeping.
- Account Clerk Certification, Kings River Community College, 2010.
- 10-key skills, good with figures and mathematics.
- Accounts payable, receivable, and journal entry experience.
- Self-motivated and dependable employee with good people skills.
- Bilingual with ability to read, write, and speak Spanish.
- Ability to successfully fit in with other staff members.

Additional information regarding my background is contained in my résumé, which is attached.

I appreciate the opportunity to apply for this position and am sure that my background and skills make me a qualified candidate. I look forward to meeting with you in the near future to answer any additional questions you might have regarding my experience and training.

Sincerely,

Patricia Singh

Enclosure

TYLER D. THOMPSON

350 N. Bates, #101 • Sacramento, CA 94208 • (559) 712-7923 • tyledt@yahoo.com

July 1, 2012

Union Pacific Transportation
Attn: Mr. Phillip Daniels
Director, Human Resources
1946 Flyway Drive
Sacramento, CA 97418

Re: PRODUCTION MECHANIC POSITION WITH UNION PACIFIC

Dear Mr. Daniels:

It is with great interest that I submit my résumé for your consideration.

After talking with Mr. Mike Williams about the responsibilities of a production mechanic, I am sure my skills and energy will meet or exceed the expectations required of a Union Pacific production mechanic.

I have operated heavy equipment and repaired hydraulic systems while working in our family business. I received training and education in PLCs and AC control circuits at Sacramento City College while enrolled in their technician program, and I believe I can be easily cross-trained in signals.

Some of the skills that I possess include:

Hydraulics - Troubleshoot and repair of Sunstrand, Rex-Roth & Eaton hydrostatic drive systems, variable displacement closed-loop systems, and constant displacement open-loop systems.

Welding - Experienced in stick, MIG & TIG, mild steel and stainless.

Electrical - Repair of electrical motors and machines.

Diesel Engines - Possess basic knowledge of diesel engines.

Please refer to my résumé for more detailed information regarding my experience, training, and education.

I look forward to meeting with you for a personal interview where I can demonstrate my skills and comment further on my education and experience.

Sincerely,

Tyler D. Thompson

Enclosure

KATHLEEN N. CASTLE
1925 Bundy Lane
Clovis, California 93612
(559) 325-9484
katnc@hotmail.com

September 12, 2012

Kaiser Permanente
Staffing Services/HR Department
4785 N. First Street
Fresno, California 93726

Re: Medical Records Analyst position

This letter is in response to your advertisement for a Medical Records Analyst. This position is of great interest to me as I am ready to transition my qualifications into a challenging medical records position with a respected institution like Kaiser Permanente.

In addition to my background as a Certified Medical Assistant, my experience and training has expanded to include medical records analysis and participation in FDA investigational studies. I am involved daily in documenting surgery studies and transmitting study data to the FDA. I possess substantial experience and education in ICD-9&10/CPT coding and classification of diseases.

I have completed the necessary course work at Merced College to become an Accredited Records Technician, and my certification will be awarded upon the completion of my clinical hours.

Along with good decision-making ability, I am highly organized and computer proficient. I am confident of my skills and believe I am a viable candidate for this position. Please review the attached résumé for additional information regarding my training and experience.

Thank you for your consideration. I appreciate your time in reviewing my qualifications and look forward to speaking with you at your earliest convenience.

Sincerely,

Kathleen N. Castle

Enclosure

MARTIN P. BROOKS
1485 N. Sussex Drive
Elmwood, Illinois 98716
(312) 864-2922
mpbrooks@yahoo.com

July 29, 2012

Mr. George Epstein, President
Well-Built Cabinet Systems
8671 E. Pontiac Boulevard
Chicago, Illinois 98711

Dear Mr. Epstein:

At the suggestion of Mr. James Archer, I am writing to express my interest in the position of Apprentice Cabinet Maker. Mr. Archer thought you might be interested in my background and training.

While attending Meader Technical College, I worked part-time for Home Depot where I sold ready-made and custom cabinets for kitchen and bathroom remodeling projects. This experience enabled me to gain an understanding of the features customers really want in cabinets for their homes. In addition, I recently completed the Cabinetmaking Technology and Milling Program at Meader College where I studied:

- cabinet design, layout, construction (inlaying, veneering, laminates, caning), and finishing
- reading blueprints, cost calculation, estimating; use and maintenance of joiners, planers, sanders, and lathes
- furniture restoration, machine woodworking, and use of CAD software

To put these skills to work in a respected firm such as yours is just the opportunity I am seeking. Please review the attached résumé and contact me at the above number so we can schedule a time to meet.

Cordially

Martin P. Brooks

Enclosure

EXERCISE 7.1

WRITING A COVER LETTER

Obtain a job announcement for a position in which you are interested. This announcement can be found at the placement center of the college where you received your training, a job board or company website, a state employment office, the human resources office of a major employer within your community, or in the Sunday edition of a local or major newspaper.

Use the same heading as appears on your résumé. Place the heading for the letter on the fourth line from the top of the page, not the seventh line as is the case for a résumé. The letter should be single-spaced with a double space (one blank line) between paragraphs. The amount of space before and after the date depends on the letter's length. The left and right margins of the letter are usually one inch, but may be greater if the letter is quite short. Use a left-justified format. Remember, when the letter is finished it should look centered on the page. You can accomplish this by adjusting the blank spaces between the date and the address and sometimes making the left and right margins larger (refer to examples of cover letters on previous pages).

Write a draft of your cover letter using either a blank sheet of paper or preferably a word processing program. Refer to the examples on the preceding pages frequently. We suggest the following steps:

1. Begin by creating a letterhead beginning on the fourth line from the top of the paper, using the same heading as appears on your résumé. Then insert a horizontal line similar to those shown in the examples on the preceding pages.
2. Insert the current date.
3. Write the name and address of the individual or department to whom you are writing. Be sure the names are spelled correctly.
4. When writing the first paragraph, be sure to state the position for which you are applying and mention something positive regarding yourself and/or the company.
5. Compose the second paragraph mentioning your best qualifications as they relate to the job for which you are applying. At the conclusion of this paragraph, mention that more details regarding education and experience may be found in the résumé.
6. Tactfully ask for an interview in the last paragraph.
7. On the second line after the last paragraph, sign off with any *one* of the following: *sincerely, cordially,* or *respectfully.*
8. Space down four lines, three blank lines, and type your full name.
9. Space down two more lines and type the word "Enclosure." This tells the reader that you are enclosing something, in this instance your résumé.
10. Sign your name above your typed name using black ink.

CHAPTER 8

References, Attachments, Salary Histories, and Employment Applications

Learning Objectives

1. Which of your colleagues and friends should you use as references?
2. What is the purpose of placing the word "Confidential" at the top of your résumé or other materials?
3. Why would a prospective employer be interested in your salary history?
4. What are the legal implications of a signed job application?

ADDITIONAL MATERIALS TO SUPPLEMENT THE RÉSUMÉ

Selling or marketing your talents is the major focus of *all* material prepared to accompany your résumé. Additional materials frequently submitted with the résumé and the cover letter include a reference sheet, a salary history, and attachments—sometimes collectively referred to as a *portfolio* or addenda to the résumé. Attachments are often included to provide examples or illustrations of your work. Occupations that often require attachments or portfolios showing samples of work include modeling, graphic arts, photography, writing, acting, sales, and cabinet making. Ask an instructor or professional in your chosen occupation if it is appropriate to send examples or photographs of your work with your résumé. Additionally, most employers will request that you complete a formal company application that requires your signature. This is addressed later in this chapter.

REFERENCES

Employers often request a list of references to gain information regarding your professional skills and character. You need to contact at least four people and ask each of them if they will act as an *enthusiastic* reference for you. You will want to contact your references before submitting materials to potential employers so they will be prepared when someone calls or writes to ask about you.

Whom should you list as references? Someone who knows you well enough to comment on your professional abilities and character. This will probably include teachers, employers (supervisors), counselors, long-time friends, and respected members of the community. It is best to have one from each of these categories. Be careful not to have all teachers or all friends. And be sure to include one or two supervisors, past or present.

How do you present your references? Use the same heading (your name, address, phone, and so on) that appears on your résumé and cover letters—placed on the fourth line from the top of the page as in the cover letter. Then three lines below the last line of your heading, center the word **REFERENCES**. Four lines below, type each of your references in turn. Be sure to include the *title* (Miss, Mrs., Ms., Mr., Dr., Judge), *name* (first and last), *occupation* (Sales Manager, Teacher, Business Owner), *address* (work location preferably), and *phone numbers* of individuals who will say positive things about you professionally and personally.

You should present your reference page to a prospective employer when you meet for the first interview. *Do not send it with the cover letter and résumé.* You should provide your references and special attachments to the interviewer at your initial meeting unless you are asked to submit these at an earlier time.

On the following page you will see an example of a reference page for Rafael Cortez (Figure 8.1).

Figure 8.1 References

Rafael E. Cortez

5559 E. Spruce Ave.
Clovis, CA 93621
(559) 845-9621
rec559@aol.com

REFERENCES

Mr. Percival Snoddgrass   (559) 430-4677
Owner, Bargain Mart
1219 N. Glenn Street
Fresno, CA 93722

Mr. Armando Martinez   (559) 875-8023
Teacher, Washington Union High School
1650 Lincoln Avenue
Selma, CA 93657

Mr. Phillip P. Laird   (559) 875-2190
Area Counsel, Peabody Trucking
10790 W. Shaw Avenue, Suite A
Fowler, CA 93709

Ms. Mercedes Johnson   (559) 224-1700
Supervisor, IRS District Office
1240 Butler Avenue
Fresno, CA 93722

SPECIAL ATTACHMENTS

Let us assume that you wish to apply for a position as a cabinet maker or furniture refinisher. One of the things that might impress a potential employer is the quality and creativity of your work in building or refinishing cabinets. Therefore, if you were to include with your résumé a portfolio (samples) of drawings (two or three) and several photographs of finished projects, it would permit a potential employer to see the type of cabinets/furniture that you have designed or refinished and how the end result looks in the color photographs you enclose.

Special attachments illustrating your capabilities are an effective means of communicating your talents. Candidates who provide examples of their work often stand out when compared to other applicants. Frequently, employers receive illustrations of work samples from only a few candidates.

How should you present samples or exhibits of your work? Present your work on paper with your letterhead (same as the résumé) or at least have a cover sheet attached with your letterhead on it that describes the material being enclosed or attached. All work should be labeled and professional in appearance.

SALARY HISTORY

Sometimes employers want to know your salary history. By asking how much you are currently earning or have earned in the past, the employer can determine if they can afford you. If the position you are seeking pays $15 an hour, yet your most recent salary has been $19 per hour, most likely the employer will think you will not be interested in taking a cut in pay or at the least want to discuss it with you. Most individuals seeking entry-level positions who have recently completed their schooling will probably not be asked to present a salary history. However, in the event that you are asked to provide a salary history now or some time in the future, it should be done in the format described in the following list:

1. Use the same heading as you have used on the résumé, cover letter, and references.
2. List your most recent employment, salary, and benefits; then, in reverse order, list your next most recent employment—providing a compensation and benefit history for previous jobs for the past 10 years.

Please note the example on the following page (Figure 8.2). In this example, it is assumed that Melinda Hawkins has 10 years of experience in retail merchandising and account sales. Note that the word "Confidential" is placed under the heading. This is done to indicate to the reader that the information should not be disclosed to any other sources. Sometimes the "confidential" notation is also placed on the résumé to indicate that you do not want potential employers to contact your employer, who might be upset to learn that you are seeking employment elsewhere.

COMPLETING EMPLOYMENT APPLICATIONS

Although your résumé may get you in the door and even to the interview stage, most employers will require that you complete and sign an application form for their company files. Why will they do this when you have already submitted a résumé and cover letter? The reason is that most individuals do not include every place they have worked or everything they have done on their résumé. Most of us include in our résumé positive information about our skills and character which is pertinent to the job for which we are applying. However, an employer may want to know all your work history, not

Figure 8.2 Salary History

Melinda A. Hawkins
1218 E. Blade Avenue.
Clovis, CA 93621
(559) 960-9221
mah141@aol.com

SALARY HISTORY
(Confidential)

J. C. PENNEY COMPANY - 20 stores, Regional Office, Fresno, California

Account Executive (9/2011 to Present)*
Current: $54,000 annually*
Starting: $37,000

Account Coordinator (1/2010–9/2011)
Ending: $30,000 annually
Starting: $27,000

BAILEY'S - Santa Fe, New Mexico

Counter Manager (8/2008–12/2009)
Ending: $22,000 annually
Starting: $22,000

GOTTSCHALK'S - Sacramento, California

Counter Manager (9/2006–7/2008)
Ending: $20,400 annually
Starting: $18,500

STOCKTON MERCHANDISE CENTER, Modesto, California

Counter Manager (10/2004–8/2006)
Ending: $16,500 annually
Starting: $16,500

***Benefits (as Account Executive)**
Bonus Based on Net Profit (Consistently $8,000 to $10,000 annually)
Company Vehicle
Fully Paid - Medical, Dental and Vision Insurance
401 (K)
Incentive Thrift Plan
Three Weeks Paid Vacation

just the selective and relevant information you placed in your résumé. And an employer may want an employment application because it has legal significance. Your signature stating that the information you have given regarding your current status, work history, and education is accurate and truthful has implications for later dismissal or denial of benefits if any aspect of this information turns out to be incorrect.

On the following pages are sample applications typically used by employers. One example is from the XYZ Company. Another sample is from Google, the respected search engine company. It illustrates how the application has a place to upload your résumé to the firm's human resources department. Like most employers, Google prefers that you have a specific position in mind when applying. Other employers may use a different style of application; however, the same type of information will be requested.

DO'S AND DON'TS OF COMPLETING AN APPLICATION

DO:

1. Complete an application online if available, as it will permit you to make changes while completing the form without having to erase. If you have the opportunity to save it, do so. You may wish to come back to it at a later time to add or delete information. Also print a copy for your records.
2. Obtain or print a second blank application form if you need to complete a printed application. Use the first one to practice on before making a final copy for submission.
3. Type or print very *neatly* and *legibly* the information requested on the application form.
4. Place something in every blank space or box—for some blanks you may state "not applicable."
5. Note that additional information may be requested other than that which appears on your résumé. You will need the telephone number and address for each former employer, your driver's license number, the dates you completed training programs, the total number of college units completed, and any professional license numbers, plus the date and state of issue. All employers must be included, even if it was for only a month. You will need to state your reason for leaving. If you were terminated, you will need to state this tactfully; for example "company downsized, position eliminated; company merged, workforce reduced" are all more discreet ways to say you were let go. As requested in item #7 of the attached form, you are to give more complete information on any termination in the remarks section (item #16).
6. Use additional sheets to explain items that do not have sufficient space on the form. Be sure to identify the items.
7. Sign and date the application with black ink.

DON'T:

1. State anything that is not true—this includes dates of employment, grade point averages, or degrees/certificates received.
2. Leave any spaces blank.
3. Erase to the extent that it makes the form appear dirty or messy if filling out a paper application.

APPLICATION FORMS

Figure 8.3 Application for the XYZ Company

XYZ Company Employment Application Form

Application must be completed in ink or typewritten

1. Name (print)   Last   First   Middle

2. Position applying for (Show exact title - Separate application required for each examination)

3. Mailing Address   No. and Street or P.O. Box No.   Apt. No.

City and State   Zip Code

4. *Social Security No.

___ ___

*Use of your Social Security number is voluntary. Social Security numbers are used for identification purposes only. If you do not wish to use your Social Security number we will assign you an identification number.

Home Phone:

Alternate Phone:

E-mail:

5. Applicable Experience - List your current or most recent position first.

Hours worked per week	From Month Day Yr.	To Month Day Yr.	Your Job Title: / Your Duties:	Employer's Name, Address and Telephone No.
A			Salary	Reason for Leaving:
Hours worked per week B	From Month Day Yr.	To Month Day Yr.	Your Job Title: / Your Duties:	Employer's Name, Address and Telephone No.
			Salary	Reason for Leaving:
Hours worked per week C	From Month Day Yr.	To Month Day Yr.	Your Job Title: / Your Duties:	Employer's Name, Address and Telephone No.
			Salary	Reason for Leaving:
Hours worked per week D	From Month Day Yr.	To Month Day Yr.	Your Job Title: / Your Duties:	Employer's Name, Address and Telephone No.
			Salary	Reason for Leaving:
Hours worked per week E	From Month Day Yr.	To Month Day Yr.	Your Job Title: / Your Duties:	Employer's Name, Address and Telephone No.
			Salary	Reason for Leaving:

SEE REVERSE SIDE-USE ADDITIONAL SHEETS IF NECESSARY

Figure 8.3 (Continued)

6. Have you ever been convicted or declared guilty of a misdemeanor or felony by any court?   YES ☐ NO ☐

If YES, give details in item 16. Conviction is not necessarily disqualifying. Each case will be evaluated on its own merits and its applicability to this position. FAILURE TO DISCLOSE THIS INFORMATION WILL BE CAUSE FOR DISQUALIFICATION, REMOVAL FROM LIST OR DISCHARGE FROM EMPLOYMENT.

You may omit:

A   Traffic violations for which the fine imposed was $100 or less. (Any Traffic violations over $100 must be shown.)

B.   Any offense committed prior to your 18th birthday which was finally adjudicated in a juvenile court or under a youth offender law.

C.   Any incident that has been sealed under Welfare and Institutions Code Section 781 or Penal Code Section 1203 45.

(If appointed, your fingerprints will be taken for a criminal history check. Certain positions may require a driving record check.)

7. Have you ever been terminated from any employment or ever forced to resign?   YES ☐ NO ☐

If YES, give details in item 16.

8. Are you now or have you ever been employed by the XYZ Company.   YES ☐ NO ☐

If YES, give details in item 16.

9. Are you related by blood or marriage to any person presently employed by the XYZ Company?   YES ☐ NO ☐

If YES, give name, relationship, and department in which employed.

_____

10. Do you wish to apply for veterans credits?   YES ☐ NO ☐

If YES, acceptable documentary proof of U.S. military service Form DD214 must be submitted with this application during the filing period.

11. Selective Service Registration. Federal Law requires male U.S. citizens and aliens residing in the U.S. who are ages 18 through 25 to register with the Selective Service System.

☐ A. I have registered with the Selective Service System.
My Selective Service Number is _____

(A copy of your Selective Service confirmation MUST be attached.)

☐ B. I am not required to register with the Selective Service System because I am exempt under the stated age/gender requirements.

12. Did you graduate from High School, pass the State High School Equivalency Exam., or do you possess a G.E.D. High School level Certificate?   YES ☐ NO ☐

A. Name of High School _____

B. Location of School _____

13. Colleges and Schools attended after high school.

Name and Location	Major	Total Units or Hours	Degrees Received

14. Driver's Lic. No. _____ **Expires** _____

Completion of this question is required only if the position for which you are applying requires the possession of a valid Driver's License.

15. If you possess any license or certificate, give the following information:

A. Title _____

B. License No. _____ Issuing State _____

Date Issued _____ Date Expires _____

16. Additional Remarks: (Attach extra sheet if necessary)

17. We want to know how you heard about this position you are applying for:

☐ Friend or Relative

☐ Newspaper: which one? _____

☐ Internet: which web site? _____

☐ Radio: which station? _____

☐ Other, please specify _____

CERTIFICATE OF APPLICANT (Read this statement carefully before signing): I hereby certify that all statements made on or in connection with this application, including those regarding my training, education and experience are true and complete to the best of my knowledge and belief, and I understand and agree that any misstatements or omissions of material fact herein will cause forfeiture on my part of all rights to employment by the XYZ Company.

_____   _____
Your Signature   **Date**

Figure 8.4 Application for Employment at Google

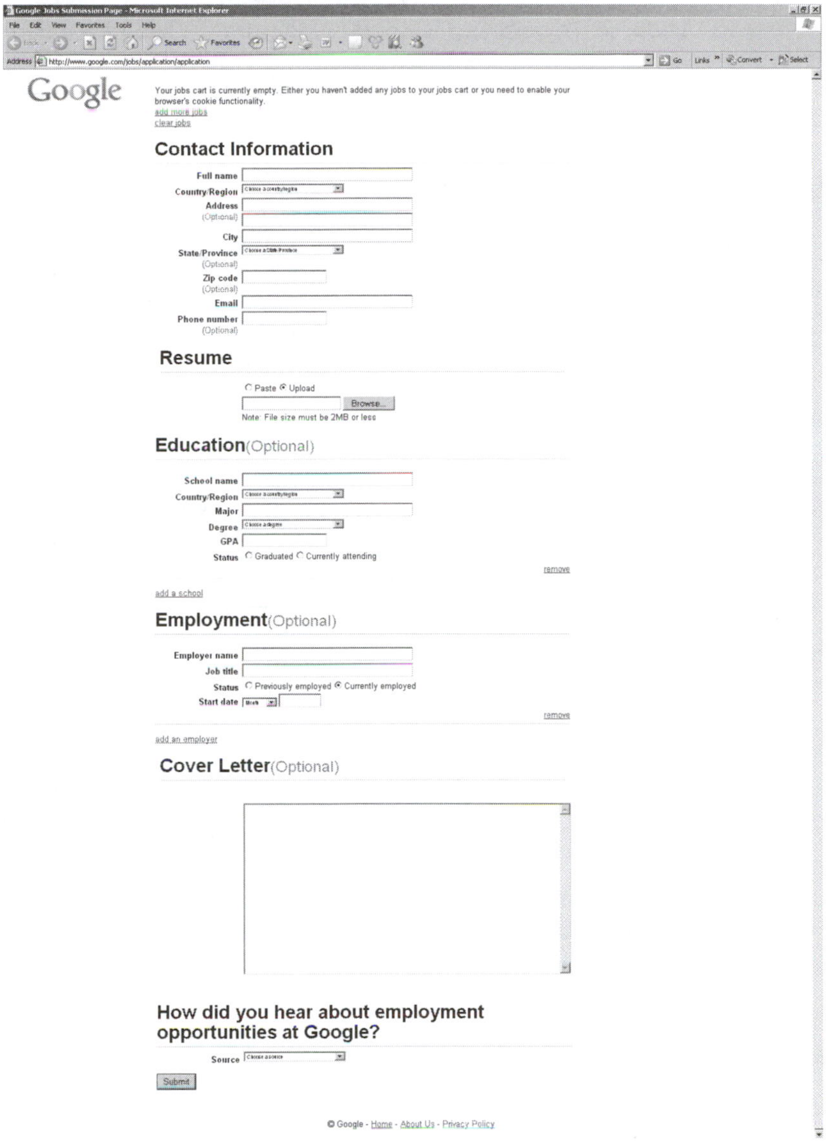

Google

Your jobs cart is currently empty. Either you haven't added any jobs to your jobs cart or you need to enable your browser's cookie functionality.
add more jobs
clear jobs

Contact Information

Full name
Country/Region
Address (Optional)
City
State/Province (Optional)
Zip code (Optional)
Email
Phone number (Optional)

Resume

Paste Upload
Browse...
Note: File size must be 2MB or less

Education(Optional)

School name
Country/Region
Major
Degree
GPA
Status Graduated Currently attending
remove
add a school

Employment(Optional)

Employer name
Job title
Status Previously employed Currently employed
Start date
remove
add an employer

Cover Letter(Optional)

How did you hear about employment opportunities at Google?

Source
Submit

© Google - Home - About Us - Privacy Policy

EXERCISE 8.1

References

List below the names of four individuals whom you will ask to act as references for you. Remember to select individuals you know from work, school, or activities within the community.

After receiving their permission to use them as references, be sure to verify the spelling of their name, title, address, place of employment, and correct address and telephone number. When you initially ask them to be a reference for you, it is a good idea to give them a copy of your current résumé. If they are asked to complete a reference form or questionnaire submitted by a potential employer, your résumé will help them provide accurate and complete information.

REFERENCE ONE:

1. Name _____
2. Title _____
3. Employer/Business _____
4. Address _____
5. Phone _____

REFERENCE TWO:

1. Name _____
2. Title _____
3. Employer/Business _____
4. Address _____
5. Phone _____

REFERENCE THREE:

1. Name _____
2. Title _____
3. Employer/Business _____
4. Address _____
5. Phone _____

REFERENCE FOUR:

1. Name _____
2. Title _____
3. Employer/Business _____
4. Address _____
5. Phone _____

Now, using the format illustrated in this chapter, place the names you have written above in a file in your word processing program. Be sure to use the same heading as on your résumé.

Résumé Submission and Follow-Up

Learning Objectives

1. Why is it a good idea to follow up an online or digital application with a portfolio containing your application materials in a printed format?
2. Who should you ask to provide letters of recommendation, and when should they be obtained?
3. What should you do 7 to 10 days after you have initially submitted your résumé?

SUBMITTING ADDITIONAL MATERIALS

As discussed in earlier chapters, it is quite common to submit your application materials online or digitally via e-mail and/or attachments. However, it is always appropriate to follow up with a hard (printed) copy of your application materials (cover letter, résumé, and any additional information). When sending print copies of the résumé to a prospective employer, we suggest the format described in this chapter.

VIA MAIL

The cover letter and résumé, plus any accompanying marketing materials, should be laser/ inkjet-printed on ivory, gray, or white paper, 24-pound classic laid. Initially it is appropriate to send *only* the cover letter and résumé unless the advertisement or job announcement requests additional materials such as references, work samples, or salary history. The reason for sending only the cover letter and résumé initially is to avoid overwhelming the employer with too many documents while he or she is in the midst of reviewing 30 to 100 application packages. However, the exception to this rule would be to include samples or photographs of your work. If you believe your work samples are outstanding, include two or three with the initial résumé and cover letter—remember, a picture is worth a thousand words.

For best results submit your application materials in a large envelope (9 × 12 inches) so the 8 ½ × 11-inch sheets of paper will not have to be folded. The *cover letter should be placed on top* and the remaining material, depending on what is being sent at the time, should be placed underneath in the following order: *résumé, references, salary history,* and *samples of your work.* The material that you enclose within the envelope should not be stapled—use a paper clip. If you fax a résumé and cover letter to an employer, be sure to follow up with a printed copy sent through the mail.

PERSONAL REFERRAL

Frequently you are referred to a prospective employer by a college or state placement office, friend, teacher, current employer, or another source. When you have the first meeting with the potential employer, it is essential that you have all of your personal employment information (résumé, cover letter, references, letters of recommendation, salary history if appropriate, and samples of your work) with you. We suggest you purchase a *twin-pocket portfolio folder* (these folders measure 9 ½ × 11 ½ inches and may be purchased at almost any office supply store). This type of folder has two pockets for placement of 8 ½ × 11-inch material, letter size, on either side when the folder is open. Purchase folders that are either dark blue or black. These colors help your cover letter and résumé stand out against the dark background. Place your signed, unfolded letter on the right side of the opened folder and the résumé on the left. Any additional documents should be placed on the left underneath the résumé in the order described in the preceding section. When you provide this material to an employer in an organized manner, you give the impression that you are well organized and plan carefully. Thus, you will stand out and be one of the few applicants—if not the only one—to do so.

OBTAIN LETTERS OF RECOMMENDATION

We suggest you have letters of recommendation available for submission to an employer. If you have previous work experience or have served an internship, it would be advisable to ask your current and former supervisors/employers to write letters of recommendation for you. The rule is: *whenever you leave a place of employment, obtain a letter of recommendation from your immediate supervisor.* The purpose of these letters is to show prospective employers what current or previous employers think of you. Assuming you have been a good employee, most employers will gladly write a letter of recommendation for you. Sometimes current and former employers ask you to write the letter and tell you that they will sign it.

What goes into a letter of recommendation? Usually the employer will state the position that you held, length of employment, your responsibilities in that position, and the positive qualities and initiative that you displayed while working for that firm. A sample letter of recommendation is given in Figure 9.1. Letters of recommendation should be given to a prospective employer at the time of the initial person-to-person contact, usually at the first interview. Of course, if the employer requested that you send letters of recommendation with the initial application, do so.

BUILD A CAREER FOLDER

Upon commencing your first job it is strongly suggested that you place a career folder in your personal files. This folder should contain copies of all employment-related information, e.g., application forms, résumés, cover letters, letters of recommendation, employer evaluations (very important), thank-you letters, and all other relevant employment documents. You will need this information the next time you want to amend your résumé or complete an application for another position. It is very important to save all of this material in a convenient place where you can easily locate it.

Figure 9.1 Letter of Recommendation

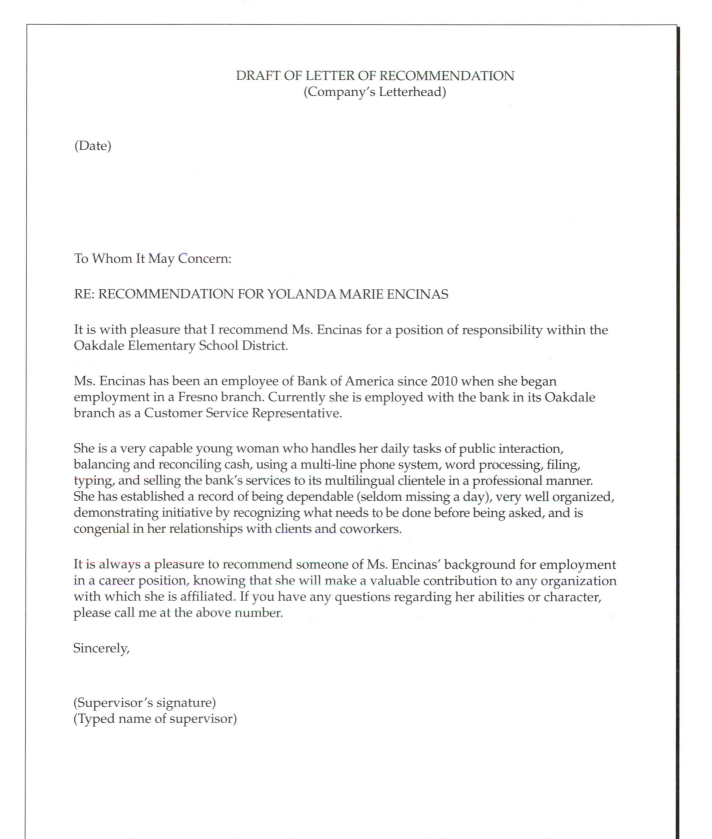

DRAFT OF LETTER OF RECOMMENDATION
(Company's Letterhead)

(Date)

To Whom It May Concern:

RE: RECOMMENDATION FOR YOLANDA MARIE ENCINAS

It is with pleasure that I recommend Ms. Encinas for a position of responsibility within the Oakdale Elementary School District.

Ms. Encinas has been an employee of Bank of America since 2010 when she began employment in a Fresno branch. Currently she is employed with the bank in its Oakdale branch as a Customer Service Representative.

She is a very capable young woman who handles her daily tasks of public interaction, balancing and reconciling cash, using a multi-line phone system, word processing, filing, typing, and selling the bank's services to its multilingual clientele in a professional manner. She has established a record of being dependable (seldom missing a day), very well organized, demonstrating initiative by recognizing what needs to be done before being asked, and is congenial in her relationships with clients and coworkers.

It is always a pleasure to recommend someone of Ms. Encinas' background for employment in a career position, knowing that she will make a valuable contribution to any organization with which she is affiliated. If you have any questions regarding her abilities or character, please call me at the above number.

Sincerely,

(Supervisor's signature)
(Typed name of supervisor)

FOLLOW-UP LETTER

Another method to make you stand out in the crowd of applicants is to *follow the submission of your résumé* with either a personal phone call or a follow-up e-mail or letter. This follow-up call or letter is something that most applicants will not do. We suggest that you write a follow-up letter to an employer or contact them by telephone to express a continued interest in the position. When you do this, you indicate to the employer that you are truly interested in the position and are persistent in seeking employment with their firm. In conversations with employers that hire frequently, we have been told often that they interview and hire applicants that are *persistent,* those who demonstrate that they really want the job.

When should you send the follow-up letter? You have to use some judgment in determining what is an appropriate time to wait before submitting this letter—it will vary depending on the company's practices. Our rule of thumb is to wait 7 to 10 days, then e-mail or mail a follow-up letter similar to the one in Figure 9.2. You will be pleased with the positive results.

Figure 9.2 Follow-Up Letter

DRAFT OF FOLLOW-UP LETTER
(your letterhead)

(date)

(inside address)

(Dear . . .)

RE: PARALEGAL POSITION

I sent a résumé to your firm two weeks ago expressing interest in a paralegal position within your practice. I wanted to indicate a continued interest in this position.

Your firm is highly respected and one with which I would very much like to be associated. I believe that I can contribute to the firm's reputation by providing a standard of performance that is of the highest caliber.

I'm sure that you have many qualified applicants. However, I urge you to again review my cover letter, résumé, and letters of recommendation. In doing so, you will find that in addition to my paralegal degree and certificate, I have:

➢ outstanding letters of recommendation from lawyers in the firm where I interned
➢ substantial experience in computerized legal research and writing (samples are available for your perusal)
➢ excellent computer and word processing skills (WordPerfect and MS Word)
➢ experience interviewing and representing clients before administrative agencies

Please call and allow me the opportunity to demonstrate and explain my qualifications more fully in a meeting at your convenience. You will be glad you made the call.

Respectfully,

Lee Ann Whitworth

CHAPTER 10

Networking and Social Networking—Where Most Jobs Are Discovered

Learning Objectives

1. What is the percentage of new job opportunities found via networking?
2. What techniques in networking were allegedly employed by both former Presidents Clinton and Kennedy?
3. What does "becoming a joiner" mean as it relates to networking?
4. Why should one be connected to, and active on, social networking sites such as LinkedIn, Facebook, and Twitter?

WHAT IS NETWORKING

Networking is using relationships, formal and informal, to learn of jobs and get inside of firms to meet hiring managers you would normally not have access to if you did not have a referral from a friend or acquaintance. When you are seeking employment, "name-dropping" will provide you with an entrance to firms, and to people within those firms, that you never dreamed you would have the opportunity to meet. The ultimate payoff from networking comes when a source says to you: "Call Tom Brannigan at Allied Industries and tell him that I referred you."

A young friend of ours, Gloria, recently related the following story about her first job in the profession of her choice, law. She was attending Cerritos Community College and working at an upscale restaurant on weekends to provide financial support. While serving a well-dressed businessman who was dining alone, Gloria made small talk about the Los Angeles Lakers basketball team and then casually asked what the restaurant guest did. He responded that he was an attorney with a practice in a nearby community. Gloria replied by saying that she was a second-year attorney assistant major at Cerritos College. Before the attorney left the restaurant, he gave Gloria his card and stated that if she were interested in part-time employment while attending school, to give him a call and he would set up an interview with his firm. Gloria called him a few weeks later and ended up going to work as a legal intern in his office while she completed the paralegal program at Cerritos College. Gloria is now a paralegal with a prominent law firm in the community where we live.

IT IS WHO YOU KNOW—TRUST US!

All of us have heard the statement: *it's not what you know, but who you know that counts.* As with most clichés, there is often a good measure of truth behind the adage. How many friends do you know who work in a family business or obtained a job through a friend of the family? Usually they obtained employment through some form of networking. They may not have taken an employment test, completed an application form, or even had a formal interview. It was their networking connection that got them in the door.

We use the same networking practice when we need to have our car repaired, need to find someone to cut our hair, or need a doctor. We ask family and friends whom they suggest for these services and with whom they have had a good experience—we ask for a recommendation, a referral. The interesting thing is that most people enjoy being asked to help with finding a doctor, an auto repair shop, or even a job. It gives them a sense of fulfillment when they can help you accomplish your goal. People usually enjoy helping others succeed at obtaining whatever they are seeking.

The greatest resource in a job search is really the people you already know or come to know while conducting your search. Networking is the path that most often gets people the job. Because of this, it is important to tell everyone you know that you are looking for a job. It may sound unoriginal, but in the real world this is how people make employment connections. A jobseeker may not be aware that the greeter at Wal-Mart with whom he works while attending college has a daughter who owns a beauty supply firm and is looking for an outside salesperson. However, if in casual conversation you discuss your desire to become a sales representative to this coworker, the subject of his daughter's firm may surface and ultimately lead to a job offer. It is quite possible that the perfect job is waiting for you within your circle of friends or family. It is up to you to let others know you are job hunting and the type of position you are seeking. This is not exploiting your family or friends; it is simply identifying what you want and being open to the possibility that the perfect job for you may be within the knowledge of your family and friends.

Research shows that many more opportunities for interviews leading to jobs or solid career opportunities result from networking than from the Internet or the classified sections of newspapers. Most sources indicate that between 65 and 85 percent of all jobs found result from networking contacts (see Tullier, *Networking for Job Search and Career Success*, 2004). Thus, you need to direct your focus and energy toward obtaining referrals that open doors and lead to satisfying employment.

The following quotation is from an article appearing in the June 3, 2008, edition of the *Wall Street Journal* as it relates to the use of networking. The author is Perri Capell, a columnist who focuses on providing career advice to job seekers.

> Through the years, I've found three issues that keep people from reaching their career objectives.
>
> Not using the right tactics to find new positions [is one]. A lot of my questions have come from job hunters who say they haven't been able to find new employment for six months or longer despite using the Internet or contacting recruiters.
>
> My advice—and that of experts—is always the same: Don't rely on the Web or on contacting recruiters. For the majority of job seekers, these are among the least effective ways to find work. You may spend all day on these activities, so you feel as though you're working hard on your search, but they're a poor use of time.
>
> *The best way to find a job is through other people.* The more people who hear about your job hunt, the faster you'll find work. Just as in sales, job hunting is a numbers game, and you need to keep knocking on doors until the right one opens.

To do this, you need to establish daily contact goals. You will want to tell each of the individuals with whom you speak about your interest in finding a job. First, identify your network of current and former coworkers, friends, family members, former classmates, professors, members of professional associations, community members, your barber, tax accountant, doctor, dentist, clergy, tradespeople, hairdresser, club members, and all their related networks.

Let your contacts know that you are exploring new opportunities and tell them specifically what type of job you are seeking. Ask each contact if she has *suggestions* on how to break into your career field—*do not ask them for a job*. Also ask them if they believe you have the skills necessary to obtain the position you are seeking and ask if they have suggestions for obtaining additional training or skills. Continue to expand your network each day. A major outplacement firm reported clients who networked the most found jobs much more quickly than clients who networked less frequently.

Here's a personal story that one of the authors, Cliff, tells about finding employment while attending college: I grew up in a rural community and after graduation planned to attend college in a nearby city, approximately 20 miles from the high school I attended. My high school basketball coach had attended the same university that I planned to attend. I told him that I was enrolling in the university the following fall, but that I would have to work while I attended college as I came from a large family with a modest income. Since most teachers, friends, family, and so on, want to help you further your education, my coach was excited about my going to college and offered some suggestions regarding part-time jobs. He said that a good friend of his was the manager of a sporting goods store near the university, and that his best friend's wife was the manager of the campus bookstore. I was excited about these prospects, especially the sporting goods store, as I had aspirations of becoming a professional baseball player at that time. With that in mind, I couldn't think of a better place to work than a sporting goods store. Well, my high school basketball coach set up an interview with the hiring manager of both of these organizations. I interviewed with each of them and began work in the summer for the sport's store and in the fall at the bookstore. I worked at the bookstore for three and one-half years—nearly all of my undergraduate college years. The manager of the bookstore even referred me to the editor of the college newspaper, who was looking for a salesperson to sell advertising. I tried that for a few months until I found out how much time was required for my studies at the university.

These contacts, my employers while in college, led to more relationships that eventually led to my position as a professor of business at a college in the community where I had lived all my life. It should also be noted that playing professional baseball was not in my future; however, a nephew, Joey Eischen, pitched in the majors for more than 10 years.

It has been proven repeatedly that it is who you know that opens doors to job opportunities that would not otherwise be accessible. Put your energies to work in identifying and contacting those in your network to uncover what is often referred to as the *hidden job market*. The name "hidden job market" stems from job openings known only to those in an organization's network. Many firms do not advertise positions initially, but seek referrals from current employees, or research candidates whose résumé they already have on file.

Before you begin contacting others, make sure you have a system to keep track of the people that you contact. You will need to develop a networking list, perhaps using Microsoft Outlook, Excel, Access, or a similar program. A networking contact form is displayed later in this chapter for possible use. Another suggestion is to prepare a 3×5-inch note card on each person you have met in your networking effort. Obtain that person's full name, job title, place of employment, business address and card, e-mail address, and telephone number, and record them. Also indicate how this person might be important to you in your job search, what information and suggestions were provided, and any personal or family information about them. Figure 10.1 shows a form you might use to track your networking contacts each week.

Former President Bill Clinton started compiling a card file on literally everyone he met during his college and law school years. He did this to create a list of those that he might want to contact at some later date—supposedly this was also a technique used by John F. Kennedy. And you can believe Clinton used these all through his political career as he was elected governor of Arkansas and president of the United States (perhaps there were a few cards he should have discarded). These networking contacts will come in handy now, and perhaps a year or two from now, when you are thinking of changing jobs and trying to remember the name of the person you spoke to about a graphic artist position in Seattle. Your fiancé is moving to Seattle, and that contact could really come in handy.

PRINCIPLES OF NETWORKING

Networking takes place in many forms, and can be both formal (for example, career fairs, employer meetings, and prearranged conversations with alumni) and informal (anyone you meet at the bank, restaurant, post office, laundromat, and so on).

- Broaden your concept of what a network is and how it works. Connections are made at odd moments, under unexpected circumstances, and often after several false starts. If a person does not work in your desired field, it does not mean that he does not know someone who does. It is a good idea to share with your present employer, even if this employer is in an unrelated field, your career goals as you near the completion of your education. Your employer/supervisor may have contacts in other industries, or your present firm may have sister companies that have occupations for which you have trained. Of course, this will depend on whether you want your present employer to know of your pending job search.

- Treat everyone you meet with respect and courtesy. In many organizations, administrative staff and receptionists who answer the phone or greet clients may also serve as "gatekeepers." They often have a lot more influence than you may think as to whether or not you will be allowed inside (the gate) to meet the hiring manager. In fact, they may even be asked for their opinion of you by their boss.

- Help others and they in turn will help you; however, when you help others, *do not expect anything in return*; just do it out of a sincere desire to be helpful or to simply do the right thing. This was brought home to us recently when a friend of more than 30 years died of cancer and named his garbage collector a beneficiary of his considerable estate. After many conversations and learning that our friend lived alone, the garbage collector invited him to join his family for Sunday dinner. A lasting friendship developed and ultimately concluded with a gift of some magnitude that was totally unexpected by the garbage man.

- Networking is a two-way street: people who help you may later ask you for assistance. *However, asking if you can provide assistance to someone who has helped you is an effective approach to marketing yourself and strengthening the networking relationship.*

Here are some specific tips:

1. Provide a copy of your résumé to everyone with whom you come in contact—either at the initial meeting or include one with a follow-up letter or e-mail. Make sure all your correspondence is well drafted in both appearance and content. Another technique is to ask networking contacts to review and make suggestions regarding your résumé's content and format. This gets them involved and causes them to look more carefully at your résumé, thus becoming better aware of your skills and abilities.

2. Do not ask the contacts for a job; ask for their ideas about where you might go or whom you might see regarding employment in the career you are seeking.

3. Prepare and memorize a 30-second summary (script) describing the type of position you are seeking and the major skills and experience that you can bring to that position. This can be crafted using the summary of qualifications from your résumé. An example using the Madeline Mosconi résumé in Chapter 4 would read as follows:

> I recently completed the Medical Assisting Front-Office Program at Heald College where I acquired skills in Microsoft Office and Medical Manager. In addition, I participated in an externship program where I spent 20 hours per week for eight weeks in a clinical setting. I was able to practice the skills I had learned by setting appointments, taking vital signs, answering

Figure 10.1 Networking Contacts

NETWORKING CONTACTS

CONTACT	OCCUPATION	PHONE	SUGGESTIONS	ADDRESS	ADDITIONAL CONTACTS	THANK YOU	RÉSUMÉ	FOLLOW-UP

telephone inquiries, making notations on medical charts, setting up examining rooms, completing laboratory forms, and calling in prescriptions. I am truly excited about entering this career field. Do you have any suggestions regarding my approach to entering this field, and would you look at my résumé to see if you think it is professional?

This script needs to be practiced at length, but delivered as though it were original. A good idea is to tape this presentation using video, audio, or both. Keep taping and reviewing it until you are satisfied that the message sounds sincere, flows naturally, and you seem confident while delivering it.

4. After you have networked with someone and asked if they know anyone who might have information about the type of employment you are seeking, send an e-mail, or, better yet, a personal handwritten note thanking them for their time and the assistance they gave you—this really stands out. This also is a good opportunity to send them a copy of your résumé if you have not done so previously.

5. About every three weeks, touch base with those in your network. Send them an e-mail, leave a phone message, drop them a note, or send them a card to let them know you appreciate their help and ask them to give you a call if they learn of anything. The "persistent wheel" gets the grease.

6. When you accept a job, notify and thank helpful contacts used in the process.

7. Use some type of tracking program or chart to keep track of your contacts. Figure 10.1 is a chart that might be of help to you.

BECOME A JOINER

We have a résumé-writing and career-coaching service in a city of over 500,000. Clients often come to us who are seeking employment after graduating from college (many seeking a position as a pharmaceutical representative—can you guess why?) or after a long work history with one firm. The number of clients who come to us and have no professional or community affiliations is surprisingly great—often they have not been members of anything! They have literally been isolated from professional and educational activities and organizations related to their occupation, and they have not developed contacts through joining community service organizations. We counsel them to join at least one professional and one community organization immediately.

Why should they join these organizations? If you are in the job market looking for employment, you need to be up to speed (current) regarding changes and new technology occurring in your career field. One way of doing this is to affiliate with a professional group dedicated to that field or occupation. The second reason is networking. For example, if you were a software programmer, it would be advisable to attend meetings of information technology (IT) professionals in your area. Through interacting with professionals at industry-related meetings, you will hear about firms that are closing, hiring, expanding, or relocating IT personnel. You will also become more knowledgeable in your field and meet people who may be able to refer you to others who are hiring. Joining needs to begin in college. Do it before graduating. The following story relates why.

Eric, a civil engineering student and officer in the university's engineering club, asked one of the authors, Cliff, to make a presentation to the student engineering group regarding résumé preparation. Eric also wisely contacted the California Department of Transportation and asked someone from their human resources department to speak to the club regarding interviewing. Eric's long-range plan, after receiving his degree, was to obtain employment with the California Department of Transportation as an engineering aide and subsequently qualify to become a licensed civil engineer. Since these jobs are highly sought after, one needs every break to get a shot at them.

The person who came out to speak to the engineering club regarding interviewing, by sheer fate, turned out to be a screener for engineering applicants at the Department of Transportation a year later when Eric applied. When this HR employee was reviewing Eric's application materials and résumé, he recognized Eric's name from their previous contacts. They had established a rapport through the numerous contacts that had occurred when Eric had asked the HR person to speak to the engineering club. I am sure this past affiliation and participation in the student organization helped Eric make the cut for the final employment interview phase. Yes, he did get the job.

SOCIAL NETWORKING

There has been a lot of buzz in recent years regarding the phenomenon of social networking. At the time this publication was being drafted, a popular film called *The Social Network,* depicting social networking and featuring one of the developers of Facebook, Mark Zuckerberg, was being nominated for an Academy Award. In early 2011, the number of users on Facebook was reported to be in excess of 800 million. The capitalization (worth) of Facebook's stock was second only to Google. Not too bad for a company and concept that began in 2004 while Zuckerberg was a student at Harvard. Why the phenomenal growth of social networking sites such as Facebook, Twitter, and LinkedIn? The nature of humans is to relate to one another—"reach out and touch someone." AT&T discovered this a long time ago and made a lot of money helping people connect. They are doing the same thing today by enabling customers to use their Internet connections, iPhones, and other digital devices to interact almost constantly with others. The means and media used to communicate with others will continue to evolve.

Should you be on one or two of these sites? Yes! An 84-year-old relative of ours is on Facebook daily to learn what his kids and grandkids are doing. They call him infrequently, e-mail him even less, but almost daily post something on their Facebook page. This lets him stay tuned to what is happening within his family.

Most of the readers of this text are probably on Facebook as it has a wide following among those under 40. The average age of LinkedIn users is reported to be 41, and the annual income $110,000. The authors suggest that you be on a minimum of two of the many social network sites. The big three at the time of this writing are Facebook, Twitter, and LinkedIn. Our belief is that you should include LinkedIn as one of the networks that you join. Why? Because it is about business and utilized by professionals, business owners, corporate executives, and nonprofit administrators. LinkedIn is considered to be the most important tool for business communication since e-mail. It is one of the first sources utilized by recruiters and HR personnel when considering candidates for a position.

RECRUITERS' AND HR'S DREAM COME TRUE

Formerly a potential employer would contact references and perform a background check on a prospective employee after several interviews and just before making a job offer. This has changed significantly. Employers now "Google" (search online) for information about every candidate they contemplate calling for an initial interview. Richard Bolles, respected career author and strategist, says "Your Google results are the new résumé." A recent survey by Jobvite (www.jobvite.com) found that 83 percent of employers now use LinkedIn, Facebook, and Twitter to find new hires, with LinkedIn being the largest with 89 percent. Recruiters/employers want to determine as much about potential employees before an interview to determine whether they are a good fit. Thus, they conduct an Internet search; a great deal of information about each of us is available online. One of the authors, Cliff, did a Google search on himself and found 1,954 hits, some going back 15 years. Guess what the first item of the 1,954 was? My LinkedIn profile.

What this means is that your digital personality needs to be professional, in good taste, and not contain any "digital dirt." It is difficult and sometimes impossible to remove negative impressions that appear online. You should do a digital search using your name and make sure that what comes up is positive and professional. If it is not, set about to change whatever you can immediately and before you commence a job search.

MORE ABOUT LINKEDIN

Some of the things that you can achieve by using and having a presence on LinkedIn include:

- Obtain information from top experts in nearly every field
- Do a complete and unique company search
- Market yourself and business if you have one
- Find other professionals and groups that have similar interests/backgrounds
- Formulate a business identity
- Expand your professional network

LinkedIn has a section in the Learning Center for job hunters (http://learn.linkedin.com/job-seekers/). LinkedIn is also partnered with "Simply Hired" (www.simplyhired.com/), which lists a wider range of job opportunities from non-LinkedIn sources throughout the United States. Simply Hired is an aggregator of job listings in the United States and internationally. It literally had three million U.S. job listings at the time this publication was being prepared. In establishing a presence on LinkedIn, it is essential to do the following:

- *Establish and/or update your profile.* It should be concise and businesslike, stating your skills, accomplishments, education, and career goals.
- *Have at least three recommendations* from those who know you in a professional context.
- *Place a current professional photograph* on your homepage.
- Adjust the privacy settings to "*Public*" on your profile.
- Make sure your profile and résumé data are the same regarding dates, etc.
- Place your LinkedIn URL in your e-mail signature block.

Your presence on LinkedIn is not complete until you have accomplished the first four items above. Naturally, you should carefully edit all content placed on your homepage—no typos or grammatical mistakes—and the writing should be well crafted. Employers are going to see this before they see you.

Remember to use keywords in your profile. As in a résumé, employers are looking for job titles and skills sets that are compatible with their needs. Use a job description of the job you are seeking to obtain the keywords for that job. Make sure your profile contains most of these keywords.

Join LinkedIn groups. There are more than 220,000 groups; surely you will find one that interests you. Consider joining alumni and trade groups. As we mentioned earlier, it is essential to be a joiner to maximize your employment and LinkedIn potential.

The principal idea of social media and LinkedIn in particular is to establish a connection (link) to someone at the company where you want to work. LinkedIn has a process to approach individuals through first-, second-, and third-degree relationships. This really means finding a friend-of-a-friend to access information, obtain an introduction, and establish new relationships. One might substitute the word "professional" for friend in the previous sentence. Remember, it is who you know and the power of information that is extremely important.

For more information and explicit directions on setting up a LinkedIn, Facebook, or Twitter account, the author suggests the source: *How to Find a Job on LinkedIn, Facebook, Twitter, MySpace, and Other Social Networks,* Brad and Debra Schepp, McGraw Hill, 2010.

FACEBOOK AND TWITTER

Yes, your presence on these online media can be valuable for obtaining employment information and disseminating information about you, your career goals, and your skills. Yes, they are more oriented toward social relationships, but if you explore each of these media you will discover sectors that focus on jobs (http://www.twitjobsearch. com/). Those active on Twitter can use *Twitres* (www.twitres.com) to display their résumé. Simply upload your résumé, and it will appear as the background on your Twitter page. Being concise in your communication skills is even more important on these two media—Twitter limits communications to 140 characters, including spaces, symbols, and punctuation. It also uses a host of abbreviations, shorthand, and terminology unique to Twitter. Facebook uses more normal language, but a lot of slang is present—be careful in all of your communications as potential employers/recruiters are going to access your communications on these media to evaluate potential candidates. A reference specifically focused on how to use Twitter in a job search is *The Twitter Job Search Guide,* Whitcomb, Bryan, and Dib, Jist Works, 2010.

EXERCISE 10.1

NETWORKING LIST

Prepare a list of 10 people whom you will contact within the next week for the purpose of networking. After identifying these 10 individuals, prepare a 3 × 5-inch note card for each with space for their name, title, firm name, place of employment, business address and card, e-mail address, telephone and fax number, suggestions they made, names they gave you, family information, and miscellaneous. In practice, you need to complete 10 networking cards each week until you find the position for which you are looking.

EXERCISE 10.2

PREPARE A LINKEDIN PROFILE

Go online and find examples of profiles on LinkedIn that describe the same occupation and skill set that you have. Then draft a LinkedIn profile using the criteria outlined in this chapter.

EXERCISE 10.3

TOOLS TO IMPROVE NETWORKING SKILLS

Extra Credit Assignment: Go to the library and check out *Networking for Job Success and Career Success*, by L. Michelle Tullier, Jist Works, 2004. Prepare a summary of the material found in Chapter 4 "Identifying and Expanding Your Network," as it relates to tools to improve your networking skills. Or select one of the social networking references listed below to prepare a report on how any of the three social networks—LinkedIn, Facebook, or Twitter—can be used to locate employment opportunities.

Reference material on social networking recommended by the authors includes:

Jacoway, Kristen, and Jason Alba. *I'm in a Job Search—Now What???*, Kristen Jacoway, HappyAbout.info, 2010.

Schepp, Brad, and Debra Schepp. *How to Find a Job on LinkedIn, Facebook, Twitter, MySpace, and Other Social Networks*. New York: McGraw Hill, 2010.

Whitcomb, Susan B., Chandlee Bryan, and Deb Dib. *The Twitter Job Search Guide*. St. Paul, MN: Jist Publishing, 2010.

11

The Interview

Learning Objectives

1. If you are asked in an interview to tell the employer about yourself, what are the essential things you should state and not state in response to this question?
2. If you are on a limited budget and need to acquire business attire for an interview, what sources are available for obtaining low-cost, appropriate clothing?
3. If you have been let go from a job, how should you respond to a question about the reason you left your previous employer?
4. Why should you take a small notebook to the interview?

TELL ME ABOUT YOURSELF

"**W**hy don't you begin by telling me about yourself?" This is one of the most frightening and frequently asked questions in the interview. Should it cause you to stutter and break out in a cold sweat? No, not if you have prepared yourself for the interview. But if you have not prepared, it could end your chances of employment with that firm.

After completing the steps necessary to prepare a top-notch résumé and cover letter, you will have gathered most of the material needed for successful interviews. The only thing remaining, as in most success stories, is to *prepare well for the interview*. This chapter will help you make plans for that first, second, and third interview. Yes, it does become easier with each interview.

TELEPHONE RECORDINGS

With the busy lives most of us lead, we have answering machines to take calls when we are not available. If you are seeking employment, you should have an answering device on your telephone or someone who communicates well taking messages for you. The message you leave on your machine or cell phone should be *concise*, contain *correct grammar*, be *easily understood*, and *have no background sounds such as heavy metal music, a baby crying, people shouting, or the dishwasher running*. An example of an appropriate message is the following:

> Thank you for calling. You have reached the Nortons; Judy and Marvin are either at school or work now. Please leave a brief message and your telephone number, and we will return your call promptly.

Another, similar message without identifying your name:

Hello, you have reached 446-8972. We are not available to come to the phone at this time. Please leave your name, number, and a brief message. We will return your call promptly.

As stated earlier, first impressions are important. Make sure your telephone message is professional in its entirety. A way to check is to have someone you respect and who is familiar with good business practices—perhaps a family member or neighbor who is in business—call your number and see if they think your message is appropriate.

WARDROBE AND HYGIENE

The rule of thumb regarding appropriate dress in an interview is to *dress as you would if you were employed in the position for which you are applying*. If you were applying for work in a business office, you would wear clothing for the interview that is similar to that worn by those within that office. When there is a question as to what is appropriate, it is usually best to dress a bit more conservatively than the most "far out" person in the office or plant.

However, there are exceptions to this rule. Sometimes uniforms are worn by employees performing the job for which you are applying; sometimes a job requires employees to appear in costume; and sometimes a work environment requires wearing coveralls or a smock. In these instances, an applicant should dress as described in the following lists.

For a *female* interview applicant, the following is suggested:

1. Business dress—a dress should be modest in length, neckline, color, and style; a business suit or pants/skirt and a blouse are fine.
2. Stockings should be worn and should complement your outfit if the attire normally worn by those in the workplace includes hosiery—if the interviewer's attention is drawn to them, they are over the top and should not be worn during the interview.
3. Shoes should be clean, polished, and in good repair—usually a *low* heel is appropriate; a stiletto heel or open-toed shoes are usually inappropriate.
4. Nails are to be modest in length and natural in color.
5. Tattoos on the arms and in other locations should be covered by wearing long sleeves or appropriate collars, and so on.
6. Minimal jewelry, such as a watch, ring, plain necklace, or pin, is in good taste. Do not wear more than two earrings per ear, nor should earrings be too large or long. Avoid noisy jewelry, such as clanging bracelets.
7. Undergarments should never be seen through or below one's outer clothing.
8. Clothing that is normally worn to parties, weddings, or a dressy social affair is not appropriate for an interview.
9. Perfume/cologne that has a slight scent and cannot be noticed more than three feet away is appropriate. If an interviewer can detect your scent, it is too strong or applied too heavily.
10. Makeup should be modestly applied.
11. Hair should be styled in a conservative manner, and long straight hair should be worn in such a way that it is not constantly being brushed back from the applicant's face during the interview.

For a *male* interview applicant, the following guidelines are suggested:

1. Clean, pressed cotton or gabardine wool pants in a conservative color are appropriate.
2. A short-sleeved sport shirt (with a collar), pressed, tucked in, and in a color that matches or coordinates with the pants is in good taste (remember, more formal

business dress is required if those on the job wear sport coats or suits and ties). Any tattoos on the arms should be covered with a long-sleeved shirt.

3. Socks should be nearly the same color as the pants (do not wear white athletic socks).
4. Casual shoes, leather or suede, low top, clean and shined are appropriate (wear more dressy shoes if wearing a suit or slacks).
5. Nails should be clean and trimmed.
6. You should be freshly shaven with hair, beard, and/or facial hair styles similar to those worn by the majority of workers in the department of the company where you are applying.
7. Use deodorant, and if you wish, *mildly* scented aftershave lotion (no strong colognes).
8. Wear minimal jewelry—a watch and one ring are okay—and modest earrings only if *commonly* worn on the job by other employees.

Piercings are fairly common; however, those that appear in the tongue and nose are still not readily accepted by the majority of employers. Our suggestion would be to remove these during the interview process, especially if you are seeking employment in a conservative environment. Often the person interviewing you will be older and more conservative than you. Thus, some of the dress or jewelry items that your friends think are cool may not be viewed the same way by the interviewer.

Obtaining appropriate clothing need not be expensive. Thrift and consignment stores frequently have good quality clothing for 20 percent of the original value. A student of one of the authors recently purchased a skirt, blouse, and dress shoes from a thrift store. The outfit looked very professional, and the price for all three items was only $12.

PLANNING FOR THE INTERVIEW

Here is a tip: When contacted by an employer to schedule an interview time, we suggest that you select a time at the end of the period when the interviews are being conducted. Some research suggests more candidates are hired from those being interviewed last or near the end of the interview process. The interviewer will remember more about you if you are at the end of the scheduled interviews, thus improving your chances for selection.

After you have made contact with an employer and scheduled an interview, you will need to do some preparation. The type of preparation will depend on the interview. The more traditional interview is a *one-on-one* situation with questions being asked by one individual, usually a representative from human resources or the supervisor of the department where you would be employed.

Another type of interview is the *panel* interview, where you are interviewed by three to five individuals who sit behind a long table and ask you questions similar to those posed in a one-on-one interview. Government agencies often use a panel interview to remove the bias that an individual interviewer might have. The panel interview always seems a bit more intimidating because the applicant is outnumbered; however, the questions are usually the same as you would normally anticipate, but asked by three or more individuals instead. The protocol for this type of interview is for you to shake hands and greet each of the interviewers upon your arrival and departure. Usually the interviewer in the center will act as the facilitator and explain the process to the applicant. In the panel interview, it is appropriate to ask the facilitator if you can hand out additional material to each of the interviewers. If given the green light, provide supplemental materials to all of those on the panel.

A third type of interview is the *telephone* or *video* interview. Sometimes, because of distance or a need to screen potential candidates, a telephone or videoconference interview will be conducted. The most important thing to remember in this type of interview is to speak clearly and in complete sentences—no "yep," "nope," or slang. And in the case of videoconferences, posture is important, as is eye contact. Otherwise, preparation for the questions to be asked will be similar to the one-on-one interview.

PRIOR TO THE INTERVIEW

First, purchase a presentation folder (twin-pocket portfolio folder as described in Chapter 9) to take with you to the interview. Place in your folder a copy of your résumé, references, letters of recommendation, and, if appropriate, samples of your work. Be prepared to leave the folder with the employer. The additional items contained in the folder will enhance your chances of being selected for the position. In addition, by preparing this folder, you demonstrate outstanding organization, planning, and presentation skills. You should also purchase a small notebook and pen to take notes during the interview. An employer may ask you to send them some additional information, for example, a college transcript. When you make a note of this in your notebook and ask for the mailing address, it again will emphasize your organization skills.

Next, be sure you know the exact location (building and office) where the interview is to be held. The day before the interview, take a practice run and see how long it takes to get there—consider traffic conditions at the time the interview is scheduled. Plan on arriving for the interview at least 10 minutes early.

When you arrive for the interview, give the receptionist your name and tell him or her the name of the person (which you have memorized) who is expecting you and the scheduled time for your interview. Anticipate a wait longer than 10 minutes. Interviews that go well often last longer than the interviewer anticipated, so the interviewer often runs past the appointed time for your interview. While waiting in the reception area before being interviewed, take out the note cards you have prepared (see the next section in this chapter, "Preparing for the Interview Questions,") for some of the anticipated questions and review them.

When you are called into the office to be interviewed, address the interviewer by name using Ms., Mrs., Mr., or Dr., and *smile*. Remember to smile frequently during the interview. Will you be nervous? Yes, of course. Does the employer expect you to be nervous? Yes. Females should offer to shake hands only if the interviewer extends a hand. Males should extend a *firm* handshake to another male, and wait until a female interviewer extends her hand.

PREPARING FOR THE INTERVIEW QUESTIONS

In preparing your answers to the questions most likely to be asked, you will need information about the company that you gathered from the Internet, a job announcement, or a company brochure (if you obtained one). The more you know about the company, the easier the interview will be.

The primary function of the interview is *to find out if you have the skills, training, experience, and interest necessary to fulfill the requirements of the position*. Most employers are trying to determine if you will fit the job and their corporate culture (company personality). The big question in the interviewer's mind is, "If you are hired, will it be a lasting employment relationship—will you remain with the employer for at least several years?" The interviewer will ask you a series of questions to try to determine if you, the job, and the company are compatible.

Some universal suggestions to those being interviewed include:

1. Smile frequently during the interview.
2. Use the name and title of the interviewer (Ms., Mrs., Mr., Dr. . . . .).
3. When you shake hands, do so firmly; grasp the entire hand, not just the fingers.

4. Wait to be asked to be seated.
5. Maintain eye contact with the interviewer (this is very important).
6. Sit up straight in the chair, do not lean on the interviewer's desk, and keep your hands still.
7. Be positive in your comments, outlook, and attitude.
8. Avoid chewing gum or tobacco, and do not bring coffee or other beverages.

It is best not to smoke or even smell of smoke during the interview—the vast majority of employers and employees do not smoke.

What kinds of questions will you be asked? On the following pages are some typical questions, and responses which we think are good answers (but not the only answers). The questions are grouped into four categories. Remember, these are only typical responses. Your responses need to be personalized to you and your qualifications.

TYPICAL QUESTIONS REGARDING YOUR QUALIFICATIONS

Note that the common thread running through all the suggested responses appearing in the following tables is to remain positive. As the cliché states, "If you are given lemons, make lemonade." Thus, if you were laid off or let go by a former employer, state that you were let go and the reason. However, follow up with a statement about what you learned from this experience (if applicable) and that you have vowed never to repeat this mistake again (if, indeed, you made a mistake).

QUESTIONS	SUGGESTED RESPONSES
1. Can you please tell me about yourself?	I've recently completed a clerical office program at Valley Community College. I took classes and completed an internship that provided me with an understanding of medical terminology, billing, scheduling appointments, and Microsoft Word. And I have an excellent letter of recommendation from Dr. Schwartz's office where I completed my 600-hour internship.
2. What are your strongest skills?	I believe my strongest skills are word processing, using either MS Word or WordPerfect. During my internship, I prepared correspondence, memorandums, newsletters with extensive graphics, and tables containing lots of numbers. I am also taking an advanced course in MS Word and Excel.
3. Why should we hire you?	By hiring me you will be getting a well-trained apprentice plumber with excellent skills, such as the ability to work with copper, steel, cast iron, and plastic pipe; and the ability to install appliances such as heaters, boilers, and air conditioners. Also you will be getting someone who wants a career position. I was with my last employer for more than four years.

4. What do you know about this job?

I downloaded a job description from the Internet. It indicated you were looking for someone (programmer and network administrator) with knowledge of C+++, COBOL, and dBASE. I am proficient in these computer languages, plus I earned Network+ and A+ Certified Technician status while completing my network technician training.

5. Will you please tell me about any work experience or training that relates to this job?

I worked part-time as a clerk/cashier for Wal-Mart while I completed the Sales Associate Program at Miller Community College. The program and part-time experience taught me to make change correctly, balance a cash drawer, greet customers politely, and make suggestions for using other services that the store provided.

6. Why do you want to work for this company?

I went on the Internet at school and found that Acme Electric is one of the fastest-growing HVAC firms in Wisconsin according to an article in *Wisconsin Business Week*. With the growth expected for this company, I see long-term opportunities and possible promotions with Acme as a heating and air control systems analyst.

7. Please describe your work experience.

(Same type of response as given for #5.)

8. Are you willing to travel in this position?

Yes, as a single woman who would like to see more of the southwestern United States, travel sounds great. In fact, I welcome an opportunity to travel and would even consider relocating to another state.

Questions Regarding Character

1. How long were you with your former employers?

All of my positions have been part-time while I was taking college classes, except in the summer when I worked full time. I have been with my present employer for 18 months, and with the previous one for about a year. I've learned a great deal in my present job. I was given a research project where I utilized case digests, Shepard's Citations, and online research systems such as Lexis.

2. What are your strengths and weaknesses?

My strengths are in my ability to work as a team member, take instruction, learn quickly, and constantly look for better ways to complete assignments. Perhaps a weakness might be that I sometimes work on a project until it's perfect. I'm beginning to realize that this is not always practical from a time management point of view.

3. Do you work well under pressure?

Yes, most of the time. When I was working as a part-time teller at a credit union while I was going to school, we were robbed by a gunman with a ski mask over his face. I kept my cool and followed all the procedures that we had been taught. We were complimented later by management for following proper procedures.

4. What are you most proud of?

When I completed the Welding Program at Paramount Vocational College, I was named the 'Trainee Most Likely to Succeed' by my classmates. It made me feel good that my buddies thought I would be successful as a welder.

5. What types of things irritate you about coworkers?

Sometimes other employees goof off when they are supposed to be working and that causes me to have to do more work. I'm beginning to learn that if I do my job well and let the supervisor handle employees who slack off, things work out best.

6. Are you comfortable working for a younger supervisor?

Yes, in fact my current boss is a woman six years younger than I am.

7. Describe your best and worst bosses.

I've not had any really bad bosses. But I have had bosses that I admire more than some of the others. The best bosses give clear instructions, let me use my initiative, are always available for questions, and tell me when I do a good job. I think I would like to be a supervisor some day.

8. What have you learned from your mistakes?

That when I make a mistake, I should admit it and try to learn from it so that I won't make the same mistake again.

9. What do you know about this company?

I called the Human Resources Department, and they sent me a brochure and annual report that told me a lot about the company. I learned that the company is selling more than 70 percent of its products on the Internet, and I feel my knowledge of creating websites and HTML would be useful in this position.

Questions Regarding Career Goals

1. What do you want to be doing in 10 years?

   I would like to be a plant maintenance supervisor. I plan to continue to take courses at the community college and within three or four years to become certified by the American Plant Maintenance Association. I have enjoyed repairing, troubleshooting, and diagnosing equipment problems all my life.

2. What are your hobbies and interests outside of work?

   Note: Mention hobbies that relate to the type of occupation you have chosen. A follow-up response after question #1 for a plant maintenance position would be:
   I have quite a collection of model cars, some of which actually can be operated by remote control. Eventually I hope to restore a 1955 Chevrolet—that's kind of my dream.

3. Do you plan to continue your education?

   Yes, in fact I have signed up to take beginning Spanish this fall.

4. What kind of work interests you most?

   Cooking. I have always been fascinated by recipes and creating special dishes for family holidays. I know this position is for a fry cook, but eventually I want to be a chef in a major restaurant.

5. What are your salary expectations for the future, say in five years?

   I believe this position pays $1800 per month to begin. When I complete my additional course work and demonstrate my skills and loyalty to this company, I would expect to earn 25 percent more in five years than when I began.

6. What motivates you?

   I imagine it's the same thing that motivates most people: doing work I like; being able to have some control over the work that I do; receiving praise for a job well done; and being paid and treated fairly.

7. Do you consider yourself a leader or a follower?

   Be honest! If you are a follower, and most people are, say something like the following:
   I'm more comfortable when others make decisions and I follow them. When I work in a team situation, I like to give my input.

8. Of the classes that you have taken, which did you like best? Why?

Naturally, this depends on your major and occupation, but the classes you indicate should be related to the type of work you want to do. An example for an advertising aide in a marketing firm would be:
Advertising was my favorite class. I really enjoyed writing ads. In fact, I worked for the school newspaper and obtained advertising material from local merchants. I helped most of them with layout and copy for the ads. That was really fun.

Difficult or Stress Questions

1. If another employee asked you to sign her out because she was leaving 45 minutes early, how would you handle this?

I would simply tell her that I wasn't comfortable doing that.

2. If your boss asks you to do some birthday shopping for her son on your lunch hour, what would your response be?

That would be tough. I would have to think about this—how well I knew the boss, whether it was a one-time thing, what kind of sacrifice it would take on my part to do this errand, and why my boss couldn't do it herself.

3. What are your greatest weaknesses?

Never say you do not have any! No one on this planet is perfect. A better way to handle this is to say something like:
Sometime I become impatient with coworkers because I want to get the job done on schedule and they goof off when the boss isn't around, but usually I try to keep my cool and just do my job regardless of what others are doing.
(or)
My writing skills are not quite as good as they should be, so I am taking an English course at the Adult Education Center in Provo this summer.

4. What do you expect in the way of a beginning salary?

Tread lightly. Try to get the interviewer to give you the range for this job. Also be sure you have done your homework and have a good idea what the job "normally" pays.
You can say:
I would assume that the pay would be based on the responsibilities, experience, and education of the individual to be hired.
(or)
The job announcement that I received from HRD said the salary range was $14 to $18 an hour, and that seems okay to me.

5. Have you ever been fired from a job?

Be honest and tactful.
No.
(or)
Yes, once when my supervisor learned that I was looking for another job. But I found another job within 10 days.
(or)
Yes, I was late for work one day at the pet store where I worked and didn't put down the correct time that I had arrived. I was let go, but given a good reference as I had been there for three years and was an assistant manager. I realized that I made a poor decision and learned from that experience.

6. What type of things do friends or family tease or criticize you about?

My sister is always kidding me about taking classes. I never seem to have the opportunity to learn all the things that I want to know about.

QUESTIONS FOR YOU TO ASK

You should ask some questions during, and at the end of the interview. You should prepare a minimum of three questions you might ask during the interview. Doing this will cause the interviewer to believe that you are sincerely interested in the position. Also, you can gain some valuable information about the job, company, and supervisors from these questions. This will help you decide whether you want to work for this company when a job offer is made. Some of the questions that are appropriate for you to ask are the following:

1. Could you describe in more detail the responsibilities of the job?
2. What skills are most critical in this job?
3. Is this a new position, or did someone leave?
4. What type of person would be most successful in this position?
5. How is an employee evaluated in this position?
6. Would it be all right for me to volunteer for a day to see what the work is really like in this department? (Your offer to volunteer will really impress most employers.)
7. What is the company's practice and attitude regarding additional training and education?
8. When might I learn of your decision regarding who is selected for this position?

AFTER THE INTERVIEW

When the interview is concluded, thank the interviewer, express an interest in the position, and ask when you might learn of the interviewer's hiring decision. Shake hands if appropriate and leave. Smile and say goodbye to the receptionist on the way out. It would help if you addressed her by name—often there is a nameplate on the desk that provides this information. Many times the interviewer will ask the receptionist what her impression was of the candidate. Thus, you may be interviewing when you are in the waiting room and not even know it. Also, ask the receptionist for a business card for the individual who just interviewed you. The address and other information on the card may prove useful later.

FOLLOW-UP LETTERS TO THE INTERVIEWER

Within 24 hours, write a thank-you letter to the interviewer. By completing this step you will stand out; most applicants do not follow up the interview with a thank-you letter. The purpose of the letter is to demonstrate courtesy, express continued interest in the position, and provide additional information regarding your qualifications that you might have forgotten to state during the interview. You can write the follow-up letter by hand or prepare it on the computer. Write the letter by hand only if you have excellent handwriting. Proofread this letter as carefully as you did your résumé.

Another thing that will make you stand out is to contact the employer approximately 10 to 14 days after the interview. The contact may be made by telephone, e-mail, or another letter: all are appropriate. This demonstrates your continued interest in the position. The letter should be short and simply state your interest and willingness to return for a subsequent interview or to answer any questions by telephone. Again, if you think of any skills or qualifications that you failed to mention during the interview, state them in the call or follow-up letter.

Figure 11.1 is an example of an interview follow-up letter for a position as a bookkeeper/accountant.

Figure 11.1 Interview Follow-up Letter

FOLLOW-UP LETTER TO THE INTERVIEW
(your personal letterhead)

(date)

(inside address)

Dear Ms. _____:

I enjoyed the opportunity to meet with you regarding the bookkeeping/accountant position that is open at Murray Equipment Supply.

One of the things that I forgot to mention to you during the interview is that last summer, while working in Yosemite National Park as a bus driver, my supervisor asked me to keep the records and schedules for the drivers. Since my boss knew that I was studying accounting, he asked if I would prepare all of the work schedules and bus routes using a spreadsheet program with which he was unfamiliar, MS Excel. Thus, I spent about three weeks using Excel to provide worksheets for more than 40 bus routes and 16 drivers. In addition, I trained my supervisor to use Excel in preparing future schedules and routes.

It is exciting to be considered for the position at Murray. I do hope that you will call me if you have any additional questions regarding my qualifications and interest in the position.

Sincerely,

(signature)

(your typed name)

EXERCISE 11.1

PERSONALIZING ANSWERS TO TYPICAL INTERVIEW QUESTIONS

Obtain a packet of 3 × 5-inch ruled note cards. Place the questions included in the sections in this chapter entitled "Typical Questions Regarding Your Qualifications," "Questions Regarding Character," "Questions Regarding Career Goals," and "Stress or Difficult Questions," on one side of the card, one question per card. On the reverse side, prepare a response that is appropriate for you, your education, experience, goals, and the position for which you will be applying. Now practice and memorize the answers that you prepared. If you do this, you will be very confident when you go in for an interview. And confidence equals success and job offers.

Résumés for Four-Year Graduates

After working for several years in the occupation for which you initially prepared, you may decide to continue your education or to seek more challenging employment with another firm. This section will discuss and provide examples of résumés for those who have completed a four-year degree (with one exception). The examples represent those seeking employment in the field in which they majored or those attempting to obtain employment after working for a few years in a career path.

For those preparing a second or follow-up résumé, the focus will more than likely be on your subsequent education or experience. After you have entered the workforce, the primary interest of future employers is how well you performed on your most recent job. Your work history becomes critical. Our suggestion is to stay with your first job for at least 18 to 24 months. This is long enough to gain experience, develop your skills, and demonstrate stability to subsequent employers.

For those with additional education, employers will look at the type of education, skills acquired, leadership activities, internships or employment, projects and/or research completed, and how well (grade point average, GPA) the applicants performed in their major.

PROFESSIONAL ASSISTANCE

As your career progresses and you are in need of more sophisticated job search materials, we offer a few suggestions. In our competitive society your cover letters and résumés are going to be competing with those of other qualified candidates. Make sure your job search materials are of a quality that places you above the competition and at the top of the interview list. If you decide to seek the services of someone more knowledgeable to assist you with the writing of your résumé, we recommend you obtain someone who has been *certified* (NCRW) and is a member of either the National Résumé Writers Association or another well-respected professional association that requires rigorous testing of those members that it certifies.

EXAMPLES OF RÉSUMÉS FOR YOUNG PROFESSIONALS

On the following pages you will find examples of résumés for those who have completed a bachelor's degree and are seeking a career position. In addition, there is an example of someone seeking a position after gaining work experience or an internship in their career field.

You will note that the formats used on these résumés differ somewhat from those illustrated earlier in this text. As you become more experienced, your résumé will also become more sophisticated. The layout of your résumé becomes even more important—it needs to be presented in a format that will make it stand out. However, the rules discussed earlier still apply—*place the experience, education, skills, and achievements most relevant to the position you are seeking at the very top of the résumé.*

Appendix A.1 Celine P. Aguilar

CELINE P. AGUILAR
2196 E. Sample Avenue
Albany, NY 12205
(518) 238-8299
CPA8600@aol.com

OBJECTIVE　REVLON ACCOUNT COORDINATOR

QUALIFICATIONS
- Six years of retail sales and management experience (3 years in cosmetics).
- Earned university degree in marketing while working full time.
- Promoted to Counter Manager in first year with Clinique.
- Team player with excellent human relations skills; effectively train and motivate consultants while maintaining high morale.
- Customer focused—proven ability to generate new business and maximize customer loyalty.
- Results oriented—consistently contribute to counter goals and company profits.
- Commended for merchandising skills and maintaining counter image.
- Excellent organizational and communication skills.

PROFESSIONAL EXPERIENCE

Macy's, Albany, NY　　　　　　　　　　　　　　　**2006–Present**

Clinique Counter Manager (2009 to Present)

- Increases in Gross Sales after assuming Counter Manager position include:
  - ✓ *Spring '11 Gift with Purchase (GWP) sales increased 19%.*
  - ✓ *Spring '10 GWP sales increased 22%.*
  - ✓ *Turnaround Cream TV Week promotion sales increased 36%.*
  - ✓ *2009 3-Step sales at 19% (up from 17%).*
  - ✓ *2009 Turnaround Cream sales at 7% (up from previous 4%).*
- Earned "Team Pro" award for highest department increase.
- Counter added a part-time consultant due to increase in business.
- Additional awards include: "3-Step Increase in Sales" and "Powder Pairs" contest (event resulted in 57% increase).

Clinique Counter Manager, Yonkers (2007–2009) (Part-time Consultant, 2006)

- Achieved "Employee of the Month" award.
- Achieved 2008 Stretch Goal with 20% increase in sales.
- Spring '07 GWP achieved 5% increase (only Albany store with an increase).
- Counter achieved 70% increase in 3-Step sales in 2007.

Sales Associate, Men's Furnishings (2006)

- Recipient of "Employee of the Month" award (2 months).
- Contest winner, annual "Jockey Sale" (Most products sold in Macy's stores).

EDUCATION　The State University of New York, State University, Albany　**2010**
Bachelor of Arts Degree in Business Administration (Marketing)
GPA 3.44

BEVERLY POLANSKI

1212 West Riverbottom
Visalia, California 93722
bevpol@aol.com
(559) 888-1642

High energy, motivated, conscientious Marketing / Public Relations Professional

Experience guiding PR and marketing functions within professional and community environments

Experience has provided strengths in:

- **ORGANIZATION / PROJECT COORDINATION**
- **PUBLIC / MEDIA RELATIONS**
- **LEADERSHIP**
- **COMMUNICATION**

PROFILE

➤ Marketing/public relations, university-trained professional experienced in development of promotional materials and events for non-profits and private sector firms.

➤ Experience producing press releases, brochures, newsletters, and radio and television material.

➤ Commended for interpersonal skills and ability to cultivate relationships within organizations and among business and community leaders.

➤ Confident, capable, and industrious—work equally well in self-directed environment and as a team member.

➤ Computer skills: Photoshop, PageMaker, QuickBooks, WordPerfect, and MS Publisher, Photo Editor, and Word.

PROFESSIONAL EXPERIENCE

Marketing/Public Relations Assistant – Part-time   *2011–Present*
ABC Marketing, Inc., Fresno, California

- Develop radio advertising scripts and negotiate contracts with stations.
- Manage client relations and firm's delinquent accounts.

Public Relations Assistant – Part-time   *2008–2010*
Tulare County Office of Education, Tulare, California

- Directed media and community communications involving the County Office of Education and area schools.
- Coordinated countywide projects and events, including Special Olympics, Teacher of the Year, Spelling Bees, Academic Decathlon and Expo, Chili Challenge, and Staff Educational Advisory Committee.

Marketing Assistant   *Summer, 2007*
Integrated Designs by FRECKLE, Fresno, California

- Planned and coordinated production of marketing materials, including video presentations and advertising brochures.
- Wrote news releases and an interoffice newsletter.

EDUCATION

Bachelor of Arts Degree, Public Relations   *2011*
California State University, Fresno

Activities:

- Head Cheerleader (3 years)
- Gymnastics (17 years – Competed Nationally)
- Dean's List, six semesters

Harold E. Fischer

2523 East Fast Avenue ▪ Fresno, California 93720 ▪ (559) 439-2481 ▪ donfisch@yahoo.com

STAFF ACCOUNTANT – PUBLIC ACCOUNTING

STAFF ACCOUNTANT with over two years' part-time experience in public accounting firm preparing corporate, individual, and partnership tax returns; assisting with audits; and preparing/organizing financial reports and supporting documentation. Professional demeanor with excellent project coordination, organization, written/oral communication, interpersonal, and analytical skills.

Accounting Expertise	**Accounting Software Applications**
‣ Tax Preparation (Corporate, Individual, Partnerships)	‣ Lacerte Tax Preparation
‣ Trust Accounting/Tax and Estate Planning	‣ Go Systems Audit
‣ Auditing – Various Business Environments	‣ BNA Fixed Assets
‣ Profit Share Accounting	‣ QuickBooks
‣ Bank Reconciliations and Bookkeeping	‣ Microsoft Excel and Word

PROFESSIONAL EXPERIENCE

WELCH ACCOUNTANCY CORPORATION, LLP, Fresno, California   **1/2010–Present**
Staff Accountant (30 hours per week) – CPA Candidate

Prepare tax returns (corporate, individual, and partnerships), property tax filings, trust and profit share accounting, and supporting financial documentation for public accounting firm with fourteen CPAs and four staff accountants.

‣ Assist with audits for diverse clientele (HUD properties and milling, agriculture, and transportation firms).
‣ Interface with clients regarding financial records required for preparing financial statements and reports.
‣ Prepare bookkeeping records, including accounts payable/receivable and journal entries.

JAMES R. NORGAN, CPA, Costa Mesa, California   **9/2009–12/2009**
Accounting Intern

EDUCATION

Bachelor of Science Degree in Business Administration; Accounting Emphasis
GPA in Major: 3.71
California State University, Long Beach, California   **2010**

CONTINUING EDUCATION IN ACCOUNTING

Spidell Publishing, Inc.
  State and Federal Tax Review   **2011**

California CPA Education Foundation
  Fast Training for Accounting and Audit   **2011**
  101 Tax Strategies of Closely Held Businesses   **2011**
  LLC, Partnerships, and S-Corporations Update and Review Workshop   **2011**

LICENSE

CPA License Examination Scheduled   **July, 2012**

Macy P. Chow

4286 North Delmont Ave., Fowler, CA 93657
(559) 916-4122 ~ mpchow@yahoo.com

CAREER FOCUS – ELEMENTARY EDUCATION

PHILOSOPHY OF EDUCATION

"I believe that I can make a difference to students by encouraging them to believe in themselves in spite of difficult circumstances. It is my goal to be a positive role model and assist students to become lifelong learners. I plan to utilize a variety of instructional methods in order to ensure that my students have the opportunity to be successful learners. I will provide encouragement and stress to them that hard work is an avenue to attaining their goals. If I am able to inspire, teach, and empower students, I will consider myself a success."

PROFILE

- Credentialed teacher (CBEST and RICA qualified) with student teaching in Clovis Unified School District.
- Developed stimulating lesson plans during student teaching assignments utilizing contextualization and SDAIE strategies in each curriculum area.
- Skilled in small-group instruction for students with learning disabilities, English as a second language, and those challenged in developing reading skills/comprehension.
- Enjoy interacting with staff and sharing ideas in a collaborative teaching environment.
- Strengths include: enthusiasm, conscientiousness, classroom organization, and technology proficiency.
- Five years of experience in customer service with expertise in effective communication, problem solving, client and staff relations, and ability to defuse volatile situations with patience and diplomacy.

STUDENT TEACHING EXPERIENCE

CLOVIS UNIFIED SCHOOL DISTRICT   1/11–6/11
    Fifth Grade (4/11 – 6/11) – Gettysburg Elementary; Mr. Fred Waring, Master Teacher
    Second Grade (1/11 – 4/11) – Gettysburg Elementary; Mrs. Laura Bush, Master Teacher

EDUCATION

NATIONAL UNIVERSITY, Fresno, CA
    Preliminary Multiple Subject Teaching Credential   2011
    Crosscultural Language and Academic Development Certification (CLAD)   2011
    Bachelor of Arts Degree in Interdisciplinary Studies   2010

FRESNO CITY COLLEGE
    Associate of Arts Degree in General Studies   2006

PROFESSIONAL EMPLOYMENT HISTORY

Senior Customer Service Representative,   Balboa Investment and Loan, Fresno, CA   **2006–2011**

COMMUNITY ACTIVITIES

- Regular participant in elementary school carnivals and fund raisers.
- Assist girls' softball team coach as needed (Southwest League).
- Thirty hours of observation and tutoring with students requiring assistance in reading and math.
- Volunteer for youth group (12–14 year olds) at Northwest Community Church.

Appendix A.5 Carla M. Pedreira

CARLA M. PEDREIRA

9713 Union Street ▪ San Francisco, California 94109 ▪ (415) 714-8642 ▪ cmp14@yahoo.com

PERSONAL PROFILE

Motivated, high-energy CAL Berkeley graduate desires opportunity to affiliate with firm that can benefit from demonstrated success providing *administrative, research,* and *marketing* support within client-focused organizations. Especially competent in settings requiring *strong project coordination, presentation,* and *communication skills.* Considered by former employers as *self-managed, and well-organized,* with an *effective balance of task- and people-oriented skills.*

EDUCATION

Bachelor of Arts Degree in Mass Communications   (GPA 3.3)   **2011**
UNIVERSITY OF CALIFORNIA, BERKELEY

Activities:
- "Service for Sight" and "Foundation Fighting Blindness," Volunteer
- "Sports for Kids," Volunteer engaged in tutoring elementary students
- Member, Delta Gamma Fraternity – Vice President and Director of Alumni Relations

Honors:
- Recipient, California Alumni Scholarship Award for Excellence in Leadership

EXPERIENCE

RESEARCH/PROJECT COORDINATION: Utilized analytical and critical thinking abilities while supporting and working collaboratively with consulting firm's legal team and financial analysts.
- Performed detailed research required in massive corporate (PG&E) bankruptcy case while employed by San Francisco consulting firm.
- Analyzed databases, files, and coded maps for California counties while collaborating with former PG&E engineers to ensure all encumbrances had been cleared prior to PG&E emerging from bankruptcy.

INTERPERSONAL/COMMUNICATION: Effectively communicated with managers, decision-makers, and clients in sales and support roles.
- Participated in developing marketing strategies, including redefining image and promotion of special events for newly renovated on-campus restaurant.
- Assisted manager of major fashion retailer in preparing regional sales presentations and worked cohesively with commission sales team in implementing marketing plan.

ORGANIZATION/ADMINISTRATION: Good writing, editing, and proofreading skills for accurate business correspondence, proposals, and reports.
- Performed administrative responsibilities and prepared claims for Central California insurance firm.

TECHNICAL SKILLS: Proficient in Microsoft Word, Excel, PowerPoint, and Access; spreadsheet development and industry-specific database software experience.

EMPLOYMENT SUMMARY

Administrative Assistant, Gonzales Consulting, San Francisco, California	**10/10–2/11**
Customer Service/Server, Bear's Lair Restaurant, University of California, Berkeley	**4/09–6/10**
Sales Associate, Nordstrom, Walnut Creek, California	**5/08–7/09**
Assistant Claims Examiner, Grover Insurance Company, Clovis, California	**Summer, 2007**

MICHAEL W. LAIRD

75 Bernard Drive West
Santa Cruz, California 93560
(831) 831-3333
mlaird@ucsc.edu

COMMUNITY ACTIVIST ♦ PROJECT MANAGER ♦ TECHNOLOGY COORDINATOR

Talented, bilingual young professional with BA Degree in Economics and Latin America/Latino Studies, plus experience organizing and coordinating UFW research projects in Central California. Seeking career opportunity where skills and dedication can promote social change and enhance people's lives. Possess experience in project organization and coordination, grant writing, developing multimedia presentations, research and writing using advanced technology and Internet resources, network administration, and web design.

Community Activism/Project Management

- Coordinated UCSC Global Information Internship Program (GIIP), placing university students (35) in community service organizations domestically and internationally. Designed curriculum and taught information technology to GIIP interns.

- Devised, researched, and implemented program to provide technology to enhance the research and networking capabilities of the UFW offices in the Watsonville, Delano, and other California sites. This entailed training staff on software and hardware applications. Placed 6 interns with UFW.

- Organized successful food drive at University of California, Santa Cruz, which produced in excess of 1,000 food items for unemployed migrant workers in the Central Coast area.

- Presently place interns with Pacific Community Advocacy Group—program is dedicated to improving housing, health, and community services for the low-income residents within the Monterey and Salinas region.

Technology Coordinator Activities

- Provided technical knowledge in setting up multi-station network for several UFW offices within Central California. In addition, provided software instruction for administrative staff.

- Member and Activist for Computer Professionals for Social Responsibility—a group taking an active role in refurbishing older technology to benefit community service (not-for-profit) organizations.

- Conducted substantial research regarding technology's impetus for economic development in third-world countries. Research focused on momentum technology provided to developing economies and the institutions within these countries.

- Created web pages for several university and community organizations.

PROFESSIONAL EXPERIENCE

Technology Coordinator, UFW, Watsonville, California	**2010 & 2011**
Instructor, Center for Global, International & Regional Studies, UCSC	**2009–2010**
Counselor/Technology Coordinator, Society & Technology Institute, UCSC	**Summer, 2008**

EDUCATION/HONORS

Bachelor of Arts Degree in Economics and Latin American/Latino Studies	**6/2011**
University of California at Santa Cruz	

Highlights: Honors Graduate and Recipient of Merrill Scholars Award
Recipient of "Outstanding UCSC Student Employee of the Year" award for 2010

PRESTON R. JEFFERSON

3029 Pacheco Avenue
Sacramento, California 95608
(916) 560-3298
871prj@gmail.com

PARALEGAL

*Articulate, poised legal professional with substantial education
and experience in procedural law and research*

SUMMARY OF QUALIFICATIONS

➢ *Education and experience:* Legal Research and Writing, Discovery and Trial Preparation, Deposition Summation, Subpoena Preparation, Litigation, Law Office Practices, Torts and Contracts, Criminal Law, Business Law, and Business Organizations.

➢ *Computer skills:* IBM computer environment with Windows and WordPerfect. Experienced in performing legal research (Internet and LexisNexis) utilizing California governmental databases.

➢ *Strengths:* Highly motivated and focused with excellent communication and organization skills.

➢ *Languages:* Bilingual: read, write, and speak fluent Spanish.

PROFESSIONAL EXPERIENCE

WEST COAST LEGAL SERVICE, San Jose, California   **2011 to Present**
Field Representative
- Maintain Fresno satellite office for service of legal documents to residents in the Central San Joaquin Valley.

MCCORMICK, BARSTOW, SHEPPARD, WAYTE, and CARRUTH, Fresno, California   **2009–2011**
Law Library Clerk
- Maintained law library, ensuring most recent cases and other legal resources were indexed accurately and included within firm's legal archives.
- Performed limited legal research and assisted staff with word processing.

FRESNO CITY COLLEGE, Fresno, California   **2005–2009**
Office Assistant - Office of Admissions and Records
- Extensive interaction with students concerning admission, financial aid, and transcripts.

DOCUMENT COPY SERVICE, San Francisco, California   **2005**
Field Representative
- Served legal documents for clients in Fresno office.

EDUCATION

Fresno City College, Fresno, California
 Paralegal - Certificate of Achievement,   **2011**

 Associate of Arts Degree in Liberal Studies   **2010**

Accomplishments:
  Dean's list 2010 and 2011
  Valley Business Conference academic scholarship recipient, fall, 2010

DAVID W. NISHIOKA
3711 N. Blackstone Avenue #112
Alameda, California 93710
(209) 226-4433
1294DN@gmail.com

BUSINESS SYSTEMS ANALYST

PROFILE

Management Background - Six years' experience in supervision involving cost control analysis, computer hardware and software maintenance, POS support, inventory control, and staff training.

University Degree - Business Administration/Information Systems Degree with projects that included systems analysis, design, and implementation for local businesses; and course work in statistical and information system analysis, management database systems, and networking.

Computer Skills - Proficient using Windows and Macintosh operating systems; *Software*: Microsoft Excel, Word, and PowerPoint. *Languages*: C++, Java, Basic, COBOL.

Strengths - Confident and well organized with strong technical, analytical, writing, and leadership skills. Excellent human relations ability—at ease with management, staff, and clients. Speak three languages— *English, Spanish, and Japanese*.

EXPERIENCE

DR. PHILLIP PATERNO, CALIFORNIA STATE UNIVERSITY, HAYWARD   *8/2011–12/2011*
Teaching Assistant
- Assisted students in compiling and analyzing data in upper division statistics laboratory course.

SUMMER BRIDGE PROGRAM, CALIF. STATE UNIVERSITY, Hayward, California   *6/2010–9/2010*
Internship, Excel Project
- Provided system support to Equal Opportunity Program Department.
- Wrote step-by-step procedural manuals for programs, installed antivirus software, and trained students in effective utilization of the Internet.

JACK IN THE BOX RESTAURANT, Oakland, California   *11/2010 to Present*
Assistant Manager
- Utilized and maintained computer system for inventory control, ordering, scheduling, financial/payroll records, and sales reports.
- Responsible for analyzing and controlling food, labor, and paper costs; forecasting; and hiring, training, supervising, and reviewing personnel.

CARL'S JR. RESTAURANT, Alameda, California   *4/2006–11/2010*
Shift Leader
- Performed daily/weekly/monthly inventory control; monitored food, paper, and labor costs; and maintained employee time records and schedules.

EDUCATION

Bachelor of Science Degree in Business Administration, *Information Systems* emphasis
California State University, Hayward; projected completion, May, 2012

Affiliations: International Business Association

Associate of Arts Degree in Business Administration
Chabot College, Hayward, California, 2009   **Honors**: Dean's List: 2008–9